AF251384

VALUable
Bible Plays
Old Testament Characters
Book 2

By
Darlene E.R. Resling

A Division of AGL Publishing
Fresno, California

VALUable Bible Plays
Book 2

Copyright ©2011 AGL Publishing
ISBN: 978-0-9674394-9-5

Published by AGL Publishing
All Rights Reserved
P.O. Box 26484 • Fresno, CA 93729 • 559-325-6679
www.aglpub.com

The purchase of this copy of VALUable Bible Plays conveys the right for performance of these works under church or school sponsorship, providing there is no charge for admission. This book may be duplicated in order to provide study parts for actors. It may not be transmitted in any form or by any means electronically or mechanically, including video recording without written permission from AGL Publishing.

Printed in the United States of America
Cover Design by Cindy Jackson

Table of Contents

Introduction

Children really do say and do the strangest things. Then too, so do adults! While a child may see the animals marching onto the ark in pears (vs. pairs), an adult might presume that Joan of Ark was Noah's wife! While these misconceptions may seem obvious and somewhat serious, both are likewise amusing.

VALUable Bible Plays are meant to be a fun way to experience God's Word for both the actors and audiences. Therefore, do not be afraid to laugh with each other throughout the rehearsals and performances. Be joyful! Proverbs 17:22 says, "A joyful heart is good medicine." All of us need that kind of medicine.

Perhaps one of the best benefits of participating in **VALUable Bible Plays** is that the God-like values-virtues-character qualities as referred to in Galatians 5:21-22, are reflected throughout each play; therefore, reinforcing and encouraging love, joy, peace, patience, kindness, goodness, faithfulness, gentleness and self-control.

With God's Word being presented in such a viable, fun and loving capacity, it would be impossible for there to be an unsuccessful practice or performance. In fact, script- line flow will encourage memorization, and emergency (forgetting the script- line) ad-libbing will not harm the message. Remember, God loves us, mistakes and all and He is the most important audience. He delights in watching His children as they share the Word in such a creative way.

Ideally, the plays will be presented in chronological order, or with a time-oriented explanation, perhaps correlating with Bible study or Sunday school lessons. Likewise, these Biblical event re-enactments will not only bring the ancient stories to life, but will enrich today's current events, along with geographical awareness.

One more thing, there are NO age limits to be involved. In fact, all of the plays are meant to include as many church participants of all ages, as possible. Parts are written for the experienced, mature actor as well as for the toddler who becomes a hopping frog in the Egyptian plague.

So, enjoy bringing the Word of God to life, inspiring all who see, hear and participate. Let your creativity flow and don't be afraid to be child-like with expectation of what God can and will do through you in **VALUABLE Bible Plays.**

Sets, Props, and Costumes

The director should feel free to alter sets, props, and stage directions to adapt for the room area or stage, cast, stage hands and technical assistants. Simplicity should be kept in mind so that all plays may be performed in a basic room with suggested backdrops and props, or on a full stage with a more elaborate setting.

Because each play is a different situation, the stage, backdrops, sets and props will likewise be different. More specific direction and/or ideas will be given at the beginning of each play.

(Ex. how to make a thundering sound) However, below are some basic examples that can be applied accordingly:

SETS

Backdrops - Tri-fold backboards can be set up to suggest a setting. Painted scenes on sheets can hang from the ceiling, attached to tall poles or draped horizontally.

Mountains - Ladders, draped in painted sheets, would give the idea. Be careful with footing. Step areas may be tacked or taped securely to the ladder.

Bodies of water - Blue, silky fabric appears as waves when moved rhythmically, either with fan blowing from off-stage or hand-held.

PROPS

Rocks - Crumbled and puffed brown wrapping paper creates easy to move rocks.

Flowers - Artificial flowers are inexpensive at dollar stores, or fields of flowers can be painted on large cardboard pieces.

Animals - Either toy stuffed or wooden animals or painted figures on large cardboard pieces will work. Also, taxidermy animals can be used.

COSTUMES

Make-up: Although make-up is not necessary, if it is available with someone to apply it, it can be fun and add some authenticity to the program.

Shirt or dress: A large pillowcase can have a head-opening cut in the bottom seam. Armholes can be cut in side seams, and the sides can be stitched in for a loose fit. Simple patterns are also available commercially. Talented designers can make professional looking costumes; they can also be rented. Different costumes will help keep characters apart, as well as to show the culture. However, costumes should not outweigh the significance of the words.

Shoes: Several sheets of sturdy cardboard, glued together can be the soles. Masking tape, wide rubber bands, or thick soft twine, attached width-wise over the foot, should hold. It is most important that shoes be checked for safety. Dark sandals are also fine.

Headband: Cardboard can be cut and stapled or strips of elastic will work. Jewels can be painted, glued or sown on. **Headdress:** A rectangular piece of cloth, pulled down longer in the back and fastened with a headband, is simple.

Wigs: Long, straight hair, or yarn glued onto brimless baseball caps will work

Booster Thoughts

Rehearsals:
1. Begin each rehearsal with a group prayer.
2. Read a relevant Bible selection as a blueprint for the play-story.
3. Verbally and/or visually present the goals to be reached during the rehearsal time.
4. In case there is a shortage of actors, some parts can be doubled. Such parts are noted with the **
5. Even though action and physical movement are involved throughout each play, safety must always be emphasized.
6. Narration is written to give clear connection between each major event.
7. Be sure to take time to thoroughly explain the story so participants know what each part entails. Remember, equally as important as the actors are to the play, so are the stage hands and technical assistants. There should always be room for everyone who wants to participate.

DAVID

I Samuel 25:1-, 31:3-6
II Samuel Ch. 1:1-27 Ch 5:1- 5, Ch 7 , 8, 18-23

CAST (Grouped by measure of involvement in play, most to least)
Double Parts: Actors can double up on these parts.

SPEAKING PARTS

Narrator: Adult - will read connecting explanations between dialogues.
David: Older student who will be made to age as the play progresses. If the optional musical ideas are used the person who will sing should have a strong singing voice. An alternate plan would be to have a singer offstage for that part while the David on stage would mouth the words.
God's Voice: Older student – The speaker would read with a strong voice, offstage.
Brother #1: Older student **
Brother #2: Older student **
2 Soldiers: Older student – These are the tattered soldiers who will report to King David from battle. The second one will carry a burlap bag with a crown.**
Servant: Older student**
Nathan: Older student or adult*
Israelite of the North #1: Older student or adult**
Israelite of the North #2: Older student or adult**
Israelite of the North #3: Older student or adult**
Absalom: Any age – This boy must have visibly long hair.**
Priests: (at least 2) Any age - One speaks. Both must be strong enough to carry the Ark.**
Mephibosheth: Any age boy – He must be able to walk with a limp.**
Audience prompters: This play is interactive! Specific people will be strategically placed within the audience with comments indicated in the script. The entire audience may be invited to interact if sufficient explanation is given before the play begins.
Farmer: Any age*
Solomon: Older male student*

NONSPEAKING PARTS

Bathsheba: Female, any age - natural looks should be stressed, no make-up**
Children of Israel: Any number, any age**
Soldiers: Any number, any age**
Sun carrier: Any age
Moon carrier: Any age
Light bulb carrier: Any age
Shadow figure: Anyone who knows how to project a shadow figure accurately

STAGE

The scenes will be enacted on the same stage. Simple props will be noted before narration.
Scenes will flow together by association with the cast's dialogue and movement.

SETTING

One background mural of the city of Jerusalem, as seen on a hilltop from a distance, is required. This would appear after David decides to make it his headquarters. An additional backdrop of trees could be used in the scene with Absalom. Other possible backdrop scenes would be sequentially projected for the short time each incident is mentioned early by the brothers as they recollect David's early life. Projections would be of Saul throwing a spear at David, Samuel anointing David, David's father receiving a note to send David and his harp to King Saul, David playing his harp for Saul, David killing Goliath, Jonathan and David as friends, David marrying Saul's daughter, Saul throwing the spear, a statue disguised as David, women singing about David, David in a cave, and David's two chances to kill Saul.

PROPS

(Simple props will be noted throughout the play)

Main Props:
- Throne-like chair for use by David, Absalom, and Solomon
- 2 staffs for Brothers #1 and #2
- Sound-effects of bleating sheep, cheering, battle sounds
- 2 crowns, one for David and one for Absalom
- A sun
- A moon
- Burlap bag with crown inside
- Oil (water) bottle
- Large stiff map of the Kingdom of the North (Israel)
- Large stiff map of the Kingdom of the South (Judah)
- Ark of Covenant chest with long handles for carrying
- A horn, a harp, a tambourine, castanets, cymbals
- A small tent
- Cloak-like robe for David during most of the play, plus a skirt- like wrap beneath the robe
- Large light bulb sign
- Two blankets
- Broomstick horse
- Long hair wig for Absalom (if necessary)
- Large farming tool for the farmer   Ex: shovel
- Numerous coins
- Small angel figure
- Large sign "YES!"
- A bright projection light to be used in shadow figure
- Baby doll

DAVID – The Play Begins

NARRATOR: It is about 1,010 years before the birth of Jesus, King Saul is dead, and all the Children of Israel are very sad. They begged God for a human king so they could be like everyone else, and God gave them Saul. Now this king is dead. The people know that during his life Saul did not live up to their great hopes. After a couple of years he disobeyed God. The prophet Samuel tried to help, but Saul just became more disobedient. Finally, God had enough, and the Spirit of God left Saul. An evil spirit came into Saul's life that changed him forever. Saul was depressed, jealous, angry, and full of hate for the rest of his life. Unfortunately, the hate Saul felt was focused on the man God had secretly chosen to replace Saul. Let's listen in as two of David's six older brothers relive David's adventures.

(Brother #1 and Brother #2 are seated cross-legged at the front of the stage, their profiles to the audience. Projections of illustrations are optional.)

BROTHER # 1: I don't know how our little brother David has been able to escape from King Saul and stay alive for so long!

BROTHER #2: I don't either, but I bet you'd have run, too, if your best friend's father started throwing spears at you! Do you remember how it all started?

BROTHER #1: I'll never forget how it all started! The prophet Samuel arrived at our home, anointed David, and left! For a while life seemed to get back to normal.

BROTHER #2: Right, normal until father got the note from King Saul asking for David to go to his court to play the harp for him. King Saul hoped David's music would make him feel better.

BROTHER #1: Then before we knew it David stood up to that nine foot tall Philistine giant named Goliath- when the soldiers were all too chicken! And he killed him with a stone from his sling- shot! Before long, David was King Saul's right hand man!

BROTHER #2: Then he became one of the king's son's best friend, good old Jonathan! David and Jonathan were as close as brothers.

BROTHER #1: David even married one of the king's daughters. Life was good for David!

BROTHER #2: Until Saul turned on him and tried to kill him!

BROTHER #1: Right- I remember the story. David had gone in to play the harp for Saul to make him feel better and Saul threw a spear right at David!

BROTHER #2: I guess David jumped away and Saul threw again! Whoa! David must have flown out of there! I sure would have been scared!

BROTHER #1: I'll never forget how David's wife helped him get away by putting a statue in the bed and dressing it with David's clothes and goat hair! The guards must have felt so foolish when they realized they had been tricked that way. *(Both brothers laugh, and then sit quietly thinking for a moment.)*

BROTHER #2: Saul seemed to change when David became so popular. You remember! Women started singing about David and how many more men he had killed compared to King Saul.

BROTHER #1: Maybe hearing David get so much credit made Saul jealous of David.

BROTHER #2: Could be.... Then again, Saul changed after his first couple of years. He seemed to ignore God. I know Samuel was really upset when Saul didn't follow God's directions more than once.

BROTHER #1: One thing I know is that I sure miss David! I can just imagine the stories he'll have to tell. The last I heard is that he's living in caves. He's desperate!

BROTHER #2: What about the reports we've heard that David actually had two chances to kill King Saul, and he refused to kill him!

BROTHER #1: A lot of people will never understand that! I'm not sure I do!

BROTHER #2: Remember that our brother David is a just and God-fearing man. I'm sure he did not want to kill the king that our God chose as king. Knowing David, he thinks God should be the one to decide who is right and who is wrong as well as who should live and who should die.

(Sounds of sheep in the distance make the brothers look in that direction. Both stand and pick up their staffs.)

BROTHER #1: Well, let's get back to work. We'll see David again. Remember, we saw Samuel anoint him; God is with David.

BROTHER #2: Yes, we have our own work to do; let's get moving!

(Both walk off stage in the direction of the sheep sounds. David runs onto the stage from the other side and stands center stage, looking around. He walks to the chair-throne and sits. Men, who are soldiers with David, come up behind him and stand straight with their arms folded.)

NARRATOR: God is with David. The Spirit of God is over David and is guiding him throughout his exile. Saul knows that things aren't right. He knows God has left him when his prayers are not answered. As the Philistine enemy approaches, Saul is so desperate he tricks a "witch" into helping him contact the Prophet Samuel, who is dead. Samuel "shows up" and tells Saul that because of his actions he, along with some of his sons, will die the next day. Time passes.

(Sounds of battle are heard, then stop. Sun and moon cross over the stage. A soldier stumbles onstage. He hobbles over to David who now sees him. The soldier kneels down in front of David.)

DAVID: Soldier! Where have you been?

SOLDIER: I was in that horrible battle with the Philistines. It was so bad we had to turn and run. So many men died. Even King Saul and his sons are dead!

DAVID: King Saul? His sons? How do you know that they are dead?

SOLDIER: I saw King Saul and he was badly wounded. He wanted to die before the Philistine soldiers killed him.

DAVID: Go on. What happened next?

SOLDIER: It was awful. The king begged his armor bearer to kill him.

DAVID: So what did he do?

SOLDIER: *(In a hesitatingly broken voice and looking around)* King Saul's armor bearer was so scared he wouldn't do it....so the king took his own sword and fell on it. *(David puts his hand to his forehead.)* Then the armor bearer fell on his own sword and died. All in the same day, the King, his armor bearer, and the king's three sons died.

(David walks to the side of the stage and falls to his knees silently crying. Lights dim, then brighten to indicate time has passed.)

(The first soldier walks off stage and soldier #2, also dirty and in ragged clothes, hobbles over to David and falls at his feet. He has a burlap bag with a crown in it. David turns, stands, and faces him)

DAVID: Where have you been?

SOLDIER #2: I have escaped from the camp in Israel. I have been in battle! King Saul and Jonathan are dead!

DAVID: What! How do you know both are dead?

SOLDIER: The army was gone, but I was there. When the king saw me he asked me to kill him, so I did! I knew he wouldn't have survived there. Then I took the king's crown. I have it here; I brought it straight to you! *(Soldier reaches into burlap bag and pulls out crown)*

(David jumps to his feet and with clenched fists pounds them in the air calls to the soldiers.)

DAVID: Soldiers! Take him away! Do away with him!

(David's soldiers drag the screaming, tattered soldier off stage. David follows but stops at the edge where he falls to his knees and covers his face as the narrator reads.)

NARRATOR: David actually already knows of Saul's death, and he knows that King Saul killed himself by falling on his own sword. The soldier's story was told to make himself look good before David, but it backfired. David is very, very upset to again hear of King Saul's death because Saul would always be God's first chosen king, anointed by God. David is also very upset because he was best friends with Jonathan, one of Saul's now dead sons. The musically talented David shares his emotions in a beautiful song called the *"Song of the Bow."*

DAVID: *(this portion may be sung or entire song in 2 Samuel 1:17-27 may be used)* "Oh Israel, your hero lies dead in the hills....The mighty have fallen...Though faster than eagles and stronger than lions... Our mighty have fallen!"

NARRATOR: Over and over David sings of how the mighty had fallen. He even orders his men to teach the song to everyone living in Judah!

(Sun and moon cross over the stage several times to show the passage of time while David sings. David walks to the edge of the stage and kneels in prayerful position.)

NARRATOR: Time passes. David asks God whether he should return to the towns of Judah; he wonders if he should return to his home headquarters of Hebron, in the southern kingdom where Abraham and his family were buried.

DAVID: Oh, God, is it time to go home?

GOD'S VOICE: Yes, David. Go to Hebron.

(David looks up towards the voice, stands, and stretches as in victory. From the other side of the stage men, women, and children come onto the stage and rush towards him while calling his name. They are carrying an oil bottle, robe, and crown.)

PEOPLE: David! David! David!

(When they reach him he again falls to his knees. One pours oil over his head, while another drapes a robe over his shoulders and another places a crown —on his head. The mood is joyful and noisy. This continues while the narrator reads.)

NARRATOR: David follows God's directions. Now 30 years old, David returns to his people. As we can see the people love David. They know that Saul turned on him after David killed the giant Goliath. They now want David as their new king of Judah. But, like other events in David's life, it isn't going to be that simple. While David is to be king in the South, there is a new king in the North, Ish-Bosheth, and a son of Saul. For 7 years David leads the people of Judah in many battles, winning them all while confusion reigns in the Northern Kingdom which is called Israel.

(The crowd around David freezes in place. Two map representations, one labeled Judah - Kingdom of the South - and the other labeled Israel - Kingdom of the North - are carried in. One person carries the Judah map, and he stands by David's group. The Israel map stands at the other side of the stage. One man holds the Israel map and speaks to the audience. Other children of Israel join him remaining quiet and attentive.)

ISRAELITE OF NORTH: *(map holder to audience)* Seven years ago we supported King Saul's son in the North. But over time King Ish-Bosheth turned out to be a foolish king. He led us into wars until he finally died! We in the north, in Israel, are ready for David to be our king. One king will rule the North and South. Do you think this is a wise move?

AUDIENCE: *(An extra carries in the yes sign and waves for the audience to scream "Yes!")*
Yes! Yes! Yes!

ISRAELITE OF NORTH #1: (*Walks over to David who is now seated on a chair-throne, which has been pushed out from the side stage and kneels.)*
David, we in the North, want you to now be our king!"

ISRAELITE OF NORTH #2: You led us in battle when Saul was alive.

ISRAELITE OF NORTH #3: And the Lord promised that someday you would rule Israel and care for us like a shepherd!

(David stands and extends his arms towards the three. All hug as narrator continues.)

NARRATOR: David agrees and is anointed after all the tribes of Israel came to him and said he should be the ruler over Israel. David made his promise with them at Hebron, before God, as he was anointed.
(David kneels and Israelite #1 takes oil bottle from his garment and pours it over David's head as he speaks.)

ISRAELITE OF NORTH #1: David! King of Israel!

DAVID: *(stands and faces audience)* I must now unite my kingdom! I know that God has truly made me king over all the children of Israel. I will move my headquarters to the city of Jerusalem. The location will help unite the two kingdoms because it is right between the kingdom of Israel in the north which has been ruled by Saul's relatives and my kingdom of Judah in the south. *(Mural of the city of Jerusalem is placed in background or projected.)*

ISRAELITE #2: *(Comes up behind David and makes aside to audience)* Not only that, but this planned spot is where a royal city was 3,000 years earlier in the time of Abraham.

NARRATOR: David and his soldiers go right to work fighting the Philistines. With God's help, they win. After one victory some of the soldiers talk about David and his plans.

(The three Israelites walk to the front of the stage and sit facing each other to talk. David walks to the side where his throne has been placed and sits quietly.)

ISRAELITE #1: David is really different from Saul. David knows God is with him and he keeps following God's commands. David continues to destroy all the idols of pagan gods he finds to remind the people of obedience to God.

ISRAELITE #2: Remember when we were told we were going to take Jerusalem? We knew that that would be a tough one!

ISRAELITE #3: I'll never forget! Jerusalem is like a natural fortress, high on a hill with deep valleys on three sides.

ISRAELITE #1: The best part was when the Canaanites in Jerusalem made fun of us because they thought we couldn't reach them! Just because they had been safe for 500 years they teased us even more!

ISRAELITE #2: Then they put blind and deaf people on guard to fight us off.

ISRAELITE #3: Weren't they surprised when we broke into their city by going underground through their water tunnel!

(All three laugh heartily)

NARRATOR: Yes, God was with David and his soldiers as they took control of the city of Jerusalem on top of Mt. Zion, around 1000 BC. As planned, Jerusalem became David's home. With a strong new wall and rebuilt buildings Jerusalem is now known as "David's City." It is stronger than ever. David knows that God has made him a powerful ruler for the good of his people. David continues to obey God. He continues to defeat the Philistines. One day, God plants another idea in David's mind.

(David stands and calls to his soldiers.)

DAVID: *(Calling with joyful command)* Soldiers! Come hear my plan. Quickly!

ISRAELITES #1, 2 and 3: *(jump up and run over to David, all speaking in unison)* Yes, your Majesty!

DAVID: *(speaking with strong conviction that increases in power as he speaks)*
We are going to get the Ark of the Covenant back from the Philistines. We're going to bring it here - to Jerusalem!

(The three Israelites kneel in front of David, then stand, cheer, clap each other on the back, and show joyful agreement. The three join David as he walks sprightly around the stage while pantomiming being on a journey. Additional audio cheering may also be heard in the background as the narrator speaks.)

NARRATOR: David knows that his kingship is different than other kings. He is directly answerable to God, the one true king. David knows that by bringing the Ark of God's Covenant to his city all the people will be reminded of their promise to be obedient to the one true God who has never left them. David knows very well who the real king is and he doesn't want the people to forget!

(While the narrator reads the Ark is carried on by two priests from a distant area of the stage. David and two priests carrying the Ark now walk towards the audience.
Additional people may play blow horns, harps, tambourines, castanets, and cymbals; the more clatter the better! David leads and is dancing wildly. He throws off his robe; underneath is a skirt-like wrap.)

DAVID: *(singing if possible)* Give thanks to our God because He is the best! His mercy on us will go on forever. Bless our Lord God forever, and ever, and ever!

(David leads the group over to a propped up picture of a tent. The Ark is placed behind it as lights dim and noise settles down. All bow heads as lights dim and the narrator reads. David puts his robe back on.)

NARRATOR: With the Ark of God's Covenant in David's city, the people remember their loyalty and obedience to God. By being in Jerusalem, it also helps unite the two countries. Peace is over the land.

(All quietly leave stage except David who returns to his throne. He holds his head in a thinking position. The light bulb prop is carried behind David. Nathan enters from the other side and David sees him.)

DAVID: *(calls to Nathan)* Prophet Nathan! Come talk to me. An idea has popped into my head. *(Nathan walks to David. David stands and points to the tent where Ark is kept)* Nathan, here I live in this fantastic palace, but the Ark of God is kept in a tent! Does that make sense to you?

NATHAN: David, God is on your side. *(Nathan faces David and puts his hands on David's head.)*

(David and Nathan go to different sides of the stage where they lie down under blankets which have been placed on the sides. Lights dim to show night, but are bright enough to see Nathan rise up when God speaks to him.)

GOD'S VOICE: Nathan! *(Nathan sits up with a start and looks in the direction of the voice.)* Nathan! Give David this message for me. *(Lights go out completely, then come back on quickly to signify day. Nathan jumps up and runs over to David who is just standing up.)*

NATHAN: *(sharply)* David! God gave me this message for you. Please listen to God's words.

(David walks quickly to his throne-chair and sits. From here he motions for Nathan to continue.)

NATHAN: God says, "David, you are my servant. Listen to my words. Why should you build a temple for me? My home has been a tent since I brought my people out of Egypt. I chose their leaders to be like shepherds. Never have I mentioned needing a special building. David, I made you leader of my people. I helped you destroy your enemies. I have given my people of Israel a land of their own where they can live in peace. I am holding the enemy back. David, I promise that your descendents will be kings. I will choose one of your sons to replace you. He will be a strong ruler, and he will be the one who will build a temple for me. I will keep my agreement and not end it like I did with Saul. One of your descendents will always be king!" *(Nathan stands silently while David walks over to the tent where the Ark is kept. He kneels and prays.)*

DAVID: Lord, I don't deserve all you have done. I don't deserve all that you promise. I am your servant, Lord. You know my thoughts before I do! You are greater than all others. You alone are God! Israel is like no other country. You made Israel famous by rescuing your people from Egypt, and then by using miracles you pushed other peoples and their gods out of the land you promised to the children of Israel. Lord, you are all powerful. You have promised great things, and I trust You. I know that You will bless my family forever!

(Stays in prayerful position)

NARRATOR: David listens to God's message and does not build a special building for the Ark. God does keep his word years later when Solomon, a son of David, replaces David as king. It is Solomon who will build a special building for the Ark of God's Covenant.

DAVID: *(He stands and walks to face audience; he speaks aloud.)* My mind never seems to rest! Lately, I've been thinking of my old friend Jonathan a lot. We were best friends, like brothers, even after his father Saul tried to kill me! I was so sorry when I heard he died with his father in battle. I've been wondering a lot recently if any of Jonathan's family is alive. Jonathan and I used to say that our kids would grow up to be best friends forever. Do any of you know? Are any members of Jonathan's family alive today?

AUDIENCE MEMBER: *(selected and prompted before the play began)* Yes! Jonathan has a son named Mephibosheth who is still alive. He is the lame one.

DAVID: Then I must find him!

(As David says this Mephibosheth hobbles onto the stage and walks haltingly towards David. David turns, sees him, and in silence walks slowly towards him until close when both stop.)

DAVID: Do not be afraid! Jonathan was your father, so I will be kind to you. I am returning everything that belonged to your grandfather Saul's family. You will always have servants and you will eat with me at my table. You will be like my own sons.

MEPHIBOSHETH: *(drops to his knees and David puts his hand on his head)*
Thank you, King David!

NARRATOR: David is true to his promise with Jonathan's son. David truly is a good man who keeps his promises. He truly loves and obeys his God...until one day.

(Mephibosheth hobbles off stage and David walks around as if trying to cool off on a hot day. A servant comes onstage and walks behind him. David suddenly stops and looks downward to give the impression that he is looking down from a roof top height.)

DAVID: *(in surprised tone)* Wow! Look at her! She's the most beautiful woman I've ever seen! *(Servant comes closer to take a look.)* Who is she?

SERVANT: The woman is Bathsheba. She is the wife of one of your army officers.

DAVID: So she's married! Well.... *(David is wearing a cloak- like robe and appears to take a piece of paper out of his sleeve and to write. He hands it to the servant.)* Here, take this to Bathsheba, now!

(Servant leaves. Bathsheba quickly comes onstage and walks over to David. They stare at each other quietly, profiles to the audience. They then turn their backs to the audience, and David extends his cloak to also cover Bathsheba. They stand quietly while the narrator reads.)

NARRATOR: David falls in love with Bathsheba. He wants to marry her so he sets Bathsheba's husband up to be killed in a battle. Not long after this a baby boy is born to David and Bathsheba. David has broken the commandments of the God he so loves and God knows it! David had done a very, very bad thing, and God is not going to let him get away with it!

(Bathsheba walks off stage and David turns to face the audience, head lowered in shame. Nathan comes onstage and walks over to David.)

NATHAN: David! God had a message for you! This is God's message: "David, I chose you King of Israel. I kept you safe from Saul. I have given you so much. Why did you break My commandments? You had a man murdered so that you could marry his wife! "

DAVID: Oh! I *have* disobeyed the Lord! *(pulls at clothes in anguish)*

NATHAN: "David! Listen to my decision! Because of this your family will NEVER live in peace. Someone in your family will cause you much trouble. You did your dirty work in secret. Well, I will make it so the trouble your family causes you will be out in the open for all of Israel to see!"

DAVID: Oh! I have disobeyed the Lord! Oh Lord, you are a kind God. Have pity on me! I have sinned and only you can make me clean. Cover my sins and create in me a clean heart. Please don't take your Holy Spirit from me! Keep me from deadly sin, and I will shout praise of you. I know that what you want is for us to feel sorrow deep in our hearts. Oh Lord, I feel that sorrow. Have pity on me!
(NOTE: This section is based on Psalm 51. A musically inclined David could sing his own rendition of the palm of repentance.)

NATHAN: Yes, David, you have disobeyed God. But David, God has forgiven you, with a catch. There will be a consequence for your wrong actions. You will live... but your baby son will die!
(Nathan leaves as David falls to the floor and sobs.)

NARRATOR: The baby son of David and Bathsheba does die. In time, an older son named Absalom, a favorite of David's, starts lots of trouble for his father, David. This happens just as God said it would, and all of Israel is watching.

(David quietly moves to the rear of the stage as Absalom jumps onstage. He strides over to address the audience.)

ABSALOM: *(to audience)* I understand your problems. But David, your king, is not interested in you! If only I could help you, I would! *(Absalom points to his chest and back at the audience as if making connections while the narrator speaks.)*

NARRATOR: This is how Absalom, a beloved son of David, turns the people of Israel against their king. Absalom tells them lies and twists the truth about his father, David, until the confused people crown Absalom king in Hebron, without David's knowledge!

(Stage hand or prompted audience participant rushes up to Absalom and places a crown (not King David's) on his head. Both run off the stage. David, Bathsheba carrying a baby, at least two

*priests, and extra family members run up on stage from the other side. They are terrified and in
a hurry. The priests are carrying the Ark of the Covenant.)*

*(The priests leave one side of the stage with the Ark while the others leave the other side.
Simultaneously, Absalom climbs on stage from another area and walks over to David's throne.
He sits.)*

NARRATOR: Absalom moves into Jerusalem and sits on David's throne. Absalom was happy
with this set-up UNTIL....

*(Soldiers jump up on stage from all sides screaming and waving weapons. Battle sounds are
heard from an audiotape.)*

NARRATOR: Absalom is happy until David's followers decide it is time to re-take the throne for
David! Now it's Absalom's turn to run for his life.

ABSALOM: *(Absalom picks up his "stick" horse and trots off stage screaming.)*
I must escape! Get out of my way! They're after me!
*(He disappears off stage. The soldiers run after him and also disappear momentarily. As soon as
he is out of sight a frightened scream is heard.)* Yeow! *(Continues screaming while narrator
reads next line.)*

NARRATOR: Absalom, in his rush, has headed for an area of trees with low hanging branches.

ABSALOM: *(off stage)* Yeow!

NARRATOR: Absalom does not lower his head enough, and his long hair gets tangled in a
branch! His mule keeps on going and Absalom is hanging in the tree by his hair!

ABSALOM: *(loudest yet)* Yeow! *(Then a blood curdling scream)* Oh no! Oh......

*(Cheers are heard off stage. The soldiers who have been chasing Absalom run up on stage and
cross over to walk off the other side while the narrator speaks.)*

NARRATOR: Absalom's cries alerted the soldiers to his location. They have found and killed the
son of King David. Absalom, the bad son who stole the throne from his father, is dead, and all
the people hear of the family tragedy.

*(The soldiers now return with David marching in front. They lead him to the throne where he
sits with little emotion. The soldiers cheer and depart.)*

NARRATOR continues: David sits on his throne and obeys God for many more years. God is
happy with King David until one day when God becomes angry over a special counting of
people that David has ordered. The people of Israel begin to suffer, so David goes to God with
his plea for the people.

DAVID: *(standing, his profile to the audience, his arms outstretched)* Oh God! The people
have not sinned; I have! Punish me! Punish my family!

(As David says the above, an angel shadow figure is cast on the back wall above the mural backdrop of Jerusalem. It looks like a large angel holding up a sword. David shows shock as he suddenly sees the figure that then disappears. A farmer with a large farm tool walks on stage and stands in the area where the shadow figure had been.)

GOD'S VOICE: David, build an altar for me where you saw the angel stand!

DAVID: *(runs over to the farmer)* I must buy your land! I must build an altar on it for our God!

FARMER: (*waving his arms)* Take it King David! It's all yours!

DAVID: No, no! I must be fair and pay you what it is worth. *(David hands over coins, and the farmer leaves the stage. David remains looking at the backdrop of Jerusalem.)*

NARRATOR: David follows God's will and the city of Jerusalem and its people are saved. In all, David rules for 40 years - 7 years over Judah, and 33 over the united kingdoms of Judah and Israel.

(As the above narration is read the shadow figure again appears with a raised sword against the backdrop of Jerusalem. The sword slowly moves down, and disappears, as does the entire shadow. David clenches his hands and bows his head in thanks.)

NARRATOR continues: David, God's second chosen king, ruled until he was old and feeble. When he gave his crown to his son Solomon, he also gave good advice.

SOLOMON: (*walks up on stage and over to David. David takes his hand and guides him to the throne. He points for Solomon to sit on the throne.)*

DAVID: Son, Solomon, it is almost my time to move on in my life. You must be brave. Remember this. Always love God and follow His directions. Do this and you will always succeed. *(David removes his crown and places it on Solomon's head. He then sits at the Solomon's feet and lowers his face. Solomon leans forward and hugs David.)*

NARRATOR: David truly was a man of God. He was the man who finished the job Joshua had begun more than 200 years earlier. Canaan, the Promised Land, is now completely under the control of the Children of Israel. The twelve tribes are on the same side. The land God had promised to Abraham, Isaac, and Jacob, had come true. But, like the first king, Saul, David eventually did fail God, his people, and himself. The difference was that David truly regretted what he had done. He knew that he alone should have suffered the punishment.

David continued to love his one true God and he let God have his way in his and his family's lives. God promised David that one of his sons would be the next king, and that he would build a temple for the Ark of the Covenant that David dreamed of building. Can life get better than this?

Would Solomon be as fair and wise a leader as his father? Might he be wiser? Would the people remember God as their true King, and not Saul or David?

Many of the Psalms were written by David. They tell of joy, remorse, and the desire for guidance. Whenever we hear a Psalm we should remember   how far God's people have come from days of exile in Egypt. Most importantly we must remember that God got them to where they are, and that God has always stayed with them and heard their cries. We know that David knew this when we read his Psalm 25:4-5, with "Make me to know your ways, O Lord: teach me your paths. Lead me in your truth, and teach me, for you are the God of my salvation; for you I wait all day long." And we know David found comfort all his days when we hear him say, "Surely goodness and mercy shall follow me all the days of my life, and I shall dwell in the house of the Lord my whole life long." Psalm 23:6.

THE END

ELIJAH
I Kings 1-21, II Kings 2, 9

CAST (Grouped by measure of involvement in play, most to least)
***Double Parts:** Actors can double up on these parts.*

SPEAKING PARTS

Narrator: Adult: The narrator will read connecting explanations between dialogues.
Elijah: Adult male: He should have long hair, wear clothes of animal skins, a recognizable cloak, and a leather belt.
God's voice: Adult or older student – This person needs to be able to read with a strong voice from off-stage.
Queen Jezebel: Adult or older girl – She will need to act haughtily.
King Ahab: Adult or older boy – He will act like a "big baby."
Solomon: Adult or older boy**
Elisha: Adult or older boy
Israelite #1: Any age**
Israelite #2: Any age**
Mothers: (2) Older girls or women**
Widow: Woman or older girl- She will express deep anger**
Rehoboam: Man or older boy – He will need to be able to sound cruel.
Prophet of Baal: (2) Older boys
Angel: Any age**
Messenger: Any age**

NONSPEAKING PARTS

Priests: (2) Any age, must be able to carry the Ark**
Messenger: Any age**
Widow's Son: Any age**
Extras: Any age**
Jug filler: Any age**
Lightning Bolt: To either be dressed as or carried as a prop**
Cirrus Clouds: Any number, any age – will be dressed as or carried as a prop**
Cumulus Clouds: Any number, any age – will be dressed as or carried as a prop**
Thunderheads: Any number, any age – will be dressed as or carried as a prop**
Raven(s): Any number, any age**
Audience "Plants": Any number, any age – will be used several times in different ways**
Flaming Horses: (2) Any age- They must be able to move easily in costume and with "broomstick" horses**
Sign Holders: Any age, as needed**

STAGE

The scenes will be enacted on the same stage. Simple props will be noted before narration. Scenes will flow together by association with the cast's dialogue and movement.

SETTING

One background mural of Mt. Carmel (which could later double as Mt. Sinai) that appears in the distance is recommended. In the beginning a sign reading "Mt. Carmel" is propped up by the mural. Loose twigs or sticks are scattered on the stage.

PROPS

(Props will be noted throughout the play)

- 12 building stones
- 12 filled jugs of water
- Ahab's robe with hood
- Ark of the Covenant (gold painted chest with 4 long handles for carrying)
- Baby doll
- Barking dogs
- Blanket
- Bread for raven to drop
- Bread loaf
- Broomstick horse heads
- Cirrus clouds
- Cumulus clouds
- Cup and plate
- Different color robes
- Hoe for Elisha
- King's throne
- Ladder draped in a gray/brown sheet to be a cave
- Large labeled map piece of Israel that fits smaller labeled map piece of Judah
- Lightning bolt attached as costume or separate
- Poster board flames
- Puffed newspaper painted "boulders"
- Pull wagon with cardboard chariot sides
- Removable cloak to go over Elijah's animal skin robe
- Set of twinkling lights or legal sparklers
- Sign reading "BAAL'S SIDE"
- Sign reading "MT. CARMEL"
- Sign reading "MT. HOREB"

- Sign reading "LORD GOD'S SIDE"
- Sign reading "JORDAN RIVER"
- Sign reading "PROVERBS"
- Sign reading "SILENCE"
- Small branches 4-5
- Smaller mural of shining white and gold temple on a brace for carrying
- Smoke/vapor effects
- Sound effects: thunder, downpours, crashes/splitting commotion
- Sticks on ground
- Thunderheads attached as costumes or carried
- Twigs
- Two bundles that represent two bulls that have been sacrificed and are ready to be put on the fire
- Two crowns that can be interchanged throughout
- Wading pool
- Wood burning/smoke scent
- Wood for two woodpiles, 4-5 logs each

ELIJAH   The Play Begins

(Solomon is sleeping on a blanket near the front of the stage. Lights are dim.)

NARRATOR: King David ruled both kingdoms of Israel for 40 years before turning the throne over to his son, Solomon. Solomon was only 20 years old at the time and willing to help rule the kingdom. One night in a dream Solomon had a chance to tell God what he wanted.

GOD'S VOICE: Solomon! Ask for anything you want, and I will give it you.

SOLOMON: Lord God, I am your servant. You have made me king in my father, David's, place. I ask that you make me wise. Teach me the difference between right and wrong; then I will know how to rule your people. *(Solomon sits on king's throne.)*

GOD'S VOICE: I am pleased with your request, Solomon. You could have asked for anything, but you asked for the wisdom to make the right decisions. Because of this I am going to make you wiser than any other king!

(Lights on full)

NARRATOR: God kept his word, and Solomon was blessed with insight and understanding. Over time it is said he wrote 3,000 wise saying and over 1,000 songs! (*A sign saying "PROVERBS" will be carried across the stage or flashed on the background*.) Solomon also knew all about plants, animals, birds, and fish. People came from all over to hear him teach. *(Extras come on stage and kneel at Solomon's feet pretending to be listening to his teachings.)*

SOLOMON: *(to crowd)* Listen to me, my people! A gentle answer turns away wrath, but a mean one stirs up anger. And remember, pride goes before destruction, and a haughty spirit goes before a fall.

NARRATOR: Solomon will always be remembered for his wise judgment with the two mothers who claimed the same baby. *(2 mothers enter, both pulling at the same baby)*

MOTHER #1: It's mine!

MOTHER #2: No, it's my baby!

NARRATOR: Solomon's decision to cut the baby in two, so each could have half, broke the lie, and the real mother offered to give the baby up. Because of her love, Solomon knew she was the true mother and gives the baby to the real mother. *(Mother #1 takes the baby, hugs it close, and walks off. Mother #2 walks, head down, off to the other side.)*

NARRATOR continues: One day Solomon remembered how his father David wanted to build a temple where God could be worshiped. Solomon had a new goal, and with God's help in 960 B.C., 486 years after God had helped the Israelites escape from slavery in Egypt, it was done! The Temple was built!

(A beautiful temple on a hand brace is carried out and placed. The crowd around Solomon stands and turns to gaze at the temple.)

ISRAELITE #1: Oh, it takes my breath away!

ISRAELITE #2: The marble, the gold, the size!

ISRAELITE #1: Look! Here comes the Ark of the Covenant that holds the Ten Commandments!

ISRAELITE #2: They're putting it in the temple! Wonderful!
(Two priests enter carrying the Ark of the Covenant. All rise and watch. Solomon walks to the front of the crowd, kneels, raises his arms in prayer.)

SOLOMON: Lord God! There is no God like you in heaven or on earth! You keep your agreements, and you are loyal to anyone who faithfully obeys your teachings! Today you are keeping the promise you made to my father David, and here is the temple in which you have chosen to be worshiped! I am your servant, and the people belong to you. You told Moses to tell the Israelites that from all the people on earth, they had been chosen to be your own. Please listen when they cry out for help! You know what is in their hearts. Answer their prayers according to their actions and what is in their hearts.
(Solomon stands and faces crowd.)

SOLOMON continues: Praise the Lord! He has kept His promise and given us peace. Every good thing God promised Moses has come true. Obey the Lord our God and follow His commands with all your heart!

ISRAELITES #1 & #2: Praise the Lord! Praise the Lord!

(All leave stage except Solomon who returns to his throne.)

NARRATOR: While his father, David, is known for uniting Israel, Solomon became the wisest and richest king in the whole world as he turned Israel into a world power with international trade. Amazing but true, Solomon had 1,400 chariots and 12,000 horsemen. He had 4,000 stalls for horses and 400 stables. His palace took 13 years to build! But it wasn't to last. Solomon made a mistake. Solomon forgot to obey God.

GOD'S VOICE: *(to Solomon who quickly turns in the direction of the voice)* Solomon! I warned you! I told you NOT to worship the gods of your wives! But you did what you wanted!
(Solomon falls to the ground and crosses his arms in anguish.) Your heart turned to other gods and you built altars on the hills surrounding Jerusalem for them!

NARRATOR: Solomon truly loved God, but his love was not perfect, and God saw what really was in his heart.

GOD'S VOICE: Solomon, I will keep my promise. You will keep your kingdom, but I will take it from your son when he is king.

NARRATOR: After 40 years of rule, Solomon died in 930 B.C., and his son Rehoboam replaced him.

(Solomon covers his face, then stands and slowly, with head bowed, walks off stage. Rehoboam enters from the opposite side wearing the same type outfit Solomon had been wearing. He walks over to the audience and speaks.)

REHOBOAM: Compared to my weak father, I will make you work harder! He used whips to punish you. Ha! *(Louder and cruelly)* I'll use whips with pieces of sharp metal! Ha Ha Ha! *(Rehoboam freezes)*

NARRATOR: As a result of King Rehoboam's harsh words, most Israelites rebelled. *(Map of Israel walks across stage)* They chose Jeroboam as king. Rehoboam continued to rule the southern area of only two tribes. The kingdom, which had been united under David and Solomon split. God's decision to take the kingdom from Solomon's family came true. While they had been strongly united, this split left both kingdoms open to attacks by powerful neighbors like the Assyrians. The Golden Age of Israel was over. Jerusalem and the Temple remained the center point of the Children of Israel. Every year the Children of Israel continued to return to Jerusalem at Passover and other holy days. Many kings ruled over the years.

(Rehoboam turns quickly and walks offstage. He can change to a different robe with a hood, or a new actor can enter as King Ahab. He struts towards the audience and stands with chest out and hands clenched on hips.)

NARRATOR continues: It is now 874 B.C. and King Ahab rules in the Northern Kingdom of Israel. He is a very, very bad man.

AHAB: Some people think I am evil! Ha! They say I've sinned more than any king before me. Well, so what! I know it must make God really angry, but I married a Phoenician princess, a pagan woman who worships Baal, not God.) Her name is Jezebel. *(The name Jezebel is hissed out to hint of evil.)* I even built an altar for Baal so we could worship together! Me worry about God? Ha! *(Raises clenched hands and stomps over to the throne to sit.)*

NARRATOR: Oh Ahab, Ahab! He thinks he is so big and strong! He really doesn't have a clue! Now here comes Elijah, prophet of the Living God, with a message for big bad King Ahab and devilish Queen Jezebel!

ELIJAH: *(walks on stage and calmly walks over to Ahab on the throne)* King Ahab! I am a servant of the one living God, the God of Israel. I swear to you, in His name, that there will be no dew on the ground or rain from the sky until I say so!

(Ahab scoffs as he stands. He leaves the stage one way; Elijah walks towards the audience but stops near the edge just as he hears the voice of God.)

GOD'S VOICE: Elijah! Leave here and cross the Jordan River. Hide near Cherith Creek. You will drink that water and eat food the ravens bring to you.

(Elijah runs towards the rear of the stage and squats pretending to scoop water up in his hands to drink. He slurps and wipes his face with his hand. A raven(s) swoops in from offstage and drops food, which Elijah picks up and eats while the narrator reads.)

NARRATOR: The ravens did bring bread and meat twice a day, and Elijah drank from the creek.... until one day. *(A dry sucking of air sound is heard as Elijah is seen dipping his hands, then turning them over to show there is no water.)*

GOD'S VOICE: Elijah! *(Elijah jumps up and faces the voice.)* Go to the town where Queen Jezebel is from. I'll have a widow there who will feed you.

(Elijah walks towards audience as the widow meanders in from the side. She is looking for sticks on the ground and bends over to pick them up as she finds them. Elijah walks up to her. A boy – the widow's son - climbs under a blanket, which was originally onstage for Solomon.)

ELIJAH: Would you bring me some water, please? *(She turns and he continues.)* And a piece of bread, too?

WIDOW: *(stops and walks back to Elijah)* I'm sorry! I'm really just out here collecting more sticks so I can cook the little bit of food I have left. When it is all gone my son and I will starve.

ELIJAH: Do not worry. Everything will be all right. Just make some bread and bring it to me. The God of Israel promises you will not run out of food before He sends rain again for the crops. *(Stays in place)*

WIDOW: *(with her hands covering her mouth, she turns and rushes to the back of the stage and freezes)*

NARRATOR: God kept his promise, but in the meantime the woman's son dies and she blames Elijah!

WIDOW: *(running up to Elijah, shouting and waving her arms as if to strike him)* My son is dead! What have I done to deserve this? I thought you were God's prophet! Did God really send you here?

(Elijah leaves her kneeling in tears and he walks over to the side where a boy and a blanket have been stretched out. Elijah kneels in prayer next to the boy.)

ELIJAH: Oh God! Why has this happened? This woman is letting me stay here and you let this happen to her son! *(Elijah leans over the boy three times as he prays.)* Lord, bring this boy back to life!

(Elijah leans back. Suddenly the boy moves. Elijah helps the boy stand up and walks him towards his kneeling mother.)

ELIJAH continues: Look! He is alive!

WIDOW: *(looks up, then jumps up, running over to her son.)* You truly are a prophet of God! Now I know for sure that you speak for the one true God!

(Both mother and son walk offstage, arms around each other. Elijah stays behind watching them.)

NARRATOR: Elijah was right. No rain fell for over three years in the north, in Samaria. During this time King Ahab and Queen Jezebel continued their sinful ways. They continued to honor Baal. They convinced others to follow Baal because the drought hurt the crops, and Baal was thought of as the "farm god." Queen Jezebel also tried to have some of God's people killed! The priests in the Southern Kingdom (Judah) worried that the other ten tribes of the Children of Israel, who lived in the Northern Kingdom (Israel) were forgetting about the God who had freed them from slavery in Egypt. They were forgetting God who had given them laws in a covenant, and who had led them to the Promised Land.

GOD'S VOICE: *(Elijah turns towards the voice)* Elijah! Go meet King Ahab! I will soon make it rain. *(Elijah turns as Ahab walks on stage. They walk towards each other.)*

KING AHAB: There you are! Are you the biggest troublemaker in Israel?

ELIJAH: King Ahab, you are the troublemaker! You and your family have disobeyed God's commands and you have worshipped the false god Baal! Now do as I say. Call everyone from Israel to meet me on Mt. Carmel and make sure all of the 450 prophets of Baal are there as well! *(Ahab walks off to the side and Elijah walks to face the audience.)*

ELIJAH continues: *(to audience)* How much longer will you people try to have things both ways? Make a choice! If the Lord truly is God, follow him! If Baal is truly God, follow him! *(A sign is held up that says "SILENCE" for the audience to see. Elijah continues, speaking earnestly)* I am the Lord's only prophet, but Baal has 450 prophets! Bring two bulls here. Let's have a test to prove whose god is the true God.

(Audience "plants" begin making positive comments about the proposed contest.)

NARRATOR: Elijah's directions were followed. Two altars were set up with wood.

(Two prophets of Baal who are seated in the audience rush up to the side of the stage and pick up wood which they carry onstage and pile up close to the front of the stage. They then stand in front of the audience.)

ELIJAH: *(facing one half of the audience. A sign is carried out and set up to show "Baal's Side" of the audience. Then Elijah places a sign that says "The Lord God's Side."* Listen to me, you prophets of Baal. Go first since there are more of you. Choose a bull, kill it, and put in on the wood, but do not set the fire. Then, I will do the same.

(The same two prophets of Baal rush to the side of the stage and quickly climb back on with a large bundle that represents the bull. They toss it on their wood pile. They remain on stage and watch as Elijah jumps offstage and hops back up with his own bundle which he tosses on his wood pile.)

ELIJAH: *(Turning between the two prophets on stage and the audience)* You prophets of Baal, listen carefully! You pray to your god Baal. I will pray to the Lord God. The god who answers by starting the fire on his altar is God! *(Cheers go up in the audience as planted prophets begin to cheer. The planted prophets then run on stage and begin to pray in front of their wood pile.)*

NARRATOR: The prophets of Baal quickly went to work. They prayed. They danced. They shouted. They did this all morning.

PROPHETS OF BAAL: *(crying out in loud desire, over and over)* Answer us Baal!"

NARRATOR: But there is only silence. Finally, at noon Elijah tried to help them.

ELIJAH: Pray louder, you prophets of Baal! Gee, Baal must be a god. Maybe he's daydreaming!
(The prophets turn to look at Elijah and clench their fists.)
Or maybe he's using the toilet! *(They growl.)* Maybe he's traveling somewhere! *(They act as if they have to hold themselves back.)* Ah, maybe he's asleep and you just have to wake him up!
(The prophets are visibly angry towards Elijah. They stomp back to their wood pile and shout louder than ever.)

PROPHETS OF BAAL: Answer us, Baal! Answer us, Baal! Answer us, Baal!

NARRATOR: All afternoon the prophets of Baal cried out. But there was no fire or answer of any kind.

ELIJAH: Look over here. The altar of the Lord is in ruins!
(Elijah picks up 12 stones from the side of the stage and places them down to build an altar.)
I am building an altar to the Lord God. Each stone stands for one of the twelve tribes of Israel; Israel being the name God gave Jacob.

(A small child's wading pool is set on the side for Elijah to bring over and place next to the altar. He then puts the wood inside the pool and then the "meat" on top of the wood.)

ELIJAH: *(Speaks to his side of the audience. He points to the jug filler.)*
You! Fill four jugs with water.

(Person rushes over to side where jugs are ready and quickly rushes over to Elijah carrying all four. Pour the water over the meat and wood. This is done making splashing sounds and fanfare.)

ELIJAH: Now do it two more times! *(This is done while the prophets of Baal look at each other and murmur.)*

NARRATOR: A whole day has gone by. Nothing has happened. It is now evening as Elijah prays.
(Lights dim down so that Elijah is barely seen.)

ELIJAH: Oh Lord, God of Abraham, Isaac, and Jacob, prove to all that you are the only God of Israel. Prove that I am your servant who has obeyed your commands. Please answer so these people will know you are the Lord God so that they will turn back to you!

(There is a crashing loud crack of lightning. The lightning bolt is carried by a runner dressed in black, which has been painted with glowing paint that reflects the special light that is cast on it. Or, a bolt could be covered with twinkling lights or sparklers to give a bright effect as it races

towards the wood. A special light effect that would signify fire, artificial electric fireplace logs, legal fireworks, or twinkling lights would then show the fire on Elijah's wood pile. The scent of burning would add to the effect. All people scream, and cry out in amazement.

While lights are still dim, a runner tosses a black fireproof covering over the wood. Lights then brighten.)

NARRATOR: The Lord God immediately answered with fire that burned up Elijah's sacrifice, wood, and stones! It was all gone!

PEOPLE ON THE LORD GOD'S SIDE: *(bow and say over and over)*
The Lord, He is God! The Lord, He is God!

ELIJAH: *(Taking command and calling to people on God's side)*
Take the prophets of Baal! Do not let any escape!

(Three earlier supporters of Elijah rush out of the audience and chase the Baal worshipers off the stage. All scream wildly.)

NARRATOR: The prophets of Baal were captured, and each one was put to death.

(Ahab comes back on stage and walks towards Elijah.)

ELIJAH: *(speaks as he approaches Ahab.)* I hear heavy rain approaching!

(Small cirrus clouds, the larger cumulus, and then dark thunderheads walk across the stage as Ahab looks with his mouth hanging open in amazement. A distant clap of thunder is heard, then a louder one, and finally a very loud crash. The sound of pouring rain and wind are heard. Elijah looks up towards the sky and puts his hands up as if to welcome the rain. Ahab pulls the hood on the back of his robe and tries to cover his face as he runs to the other side of the stage away from Elijah who walks to the side and freezes.)

NARRATOR: It was true. After three long, dry years, the drought and famine were finally over! King Ahab returns to Queen Jezebel to tell her about what had happened.

JEZEBEL: *(Walks up to meet the returning Ahab and yanks hood from the back of his head.)*
Ahab! You look like a drowned rat! What happened?

AHAB: *(Shaking himself like a wet dog)* Jezebel, I can't believe it! That Elijah – that prophet of God – held a contest to see which god – Baal or Elijah's God – would set fire to the sacrifice first *(shakes again)* and his God answered! Now it's raining for the first time in three years!

JEZEBEL: And what about my prophets?

AHAB: Elijah had all 450 of your prophets of Baal killed!

JEZEBEL: What?!! *(Looks offstage and calls)*
Messenger! Come here, now! Elijah must be stopped.

MESSENGER: *(Runs in and falls at her feet, bows up and down as if terrified of being too slow)* Yes, Queen Jezebel, what can I do for you?

JEZEBEL: Go immediately to Elijah. Tell him this from Queen Jezebel, "You killed my prophet, so I am going to kill you! May the gods severely punish me if I do not kill you by tomorrow!"

(Messenger runs offstage one way. Ahab and Jezebel depart the stage in the other direction. Elijah begins to walk in circles, holding his sides and rocking in fear.)

NARRATOR: Elijah was terrified when he received the message from vicious Queen Jezebel. He walked an entire day in the desert. Finally he saw a large bush and fell down in its shade.

ELIJAH: Oh, Lord God! Hear my cry! I've had enough. Just let me die! I'm no better than any of my ancestors. Please, just let me die. *(Elijah lies down and starts to snore; an angel enters and places bread and water jar by Elijah's head.)*

ANGEL: *(Touches Elijah to awaken him, Elijah sits up)* Eat and drink!

(Angel walks behind Elijah as Elijah eats and drinks. Elijah lies down and starts to snore again. The angel again touches him to awaken him. Elijah sits up.)

ANGEL continues: You must get up and eat so that you are strong enough for the journey. *(Angel leaves stage while Elijah eats and drinks.)*

(Elijah stands, looks in all directions, raises his arms as a sign of strength and starts walking. Sign reading "MT. HOREB" replaces the "MT. CARMEL" sign.)

NARRATOR: Elijah gets his energy back, and his nerve to continue on his journey for God, despite the threats from Queen Jezebel. He walks for forty days and forty nights until he reaches Mount Sinai. The first night there he spots a cave.

ELIJAH: *(pointing and talking to self)* Oh good! I see a cave. I'll spend the night there. *(A tall ladder draped in painted "cave" colors is the cave. It has just been pushed onstage during above narration.)*

GOD'S VOICE: Elijah! What are you doing here?

ELIJAH: *(jumping up and turning towards the voice)* Oh Lord! I have used all my strength and energy for you, Almighty God! But our people, the Israelites, have turned against you. They reject our covenant, and they break down our altars. Now they are killing your prophets. I am the only prophet left, and they are after me!

GOD'S VOICE: Leave this cave and stand on the mountain. You will be in the presence of your God because your God is about to pass by. *(Elijah runs over to the other side of the stage. When he stops, howling wind sounds are heard and large "rocks" are tossed towards him from offstage as the narrator speaks. He kneels and covers his head.)*

NARRATOR: The wind tore the mountain apart, but God was not in that wind.
(A loud splitting sound is heard which represents an earthquake.)
Then there was an earthquake, but God was not in the earthquake.
(Flicker lights. Poster board flames are walked across the stage and walk once around the kneeling Elijah before departing.)
After the earthquake was a fire, but still, God was not in the fire. Then, there was a gentle whisper, like a breeze. God gives Elijah a second chance to answer. *(Elijah stands)*

GOD'S VOICE: What are doing here, Elijah?

ELIJAH: *(covering his face with his robe and looking towards the voice)*
Oh Lord! I have used all my strength and energy for you!

GOD'S VOICE: Go back the way you came. I have 7,000 people in Israel who refuse to honor Baal. On the way back you will meet Elisha. Anoint him because he will take your place as prophet.

(Elisha comes onstage chopping the "soil" ahead of him with a hoe. Elijah walks towards him.)

NARRATOR: Elijah obeyed God. As he walks through a field he sees Elisha farming the land.

ELIJAH: *(Elijah walks up to Elisha and puts his cloak over Elisha's shoulders. Elisha drops the hoe in his hands.)* Elisha, God wants you to be the prophet who will take my place.

NARRATOR: Elisha agrees to follow Elijah, but only after he says goodbye to his parents. *(Both walk offstage and Ahab and Jezebel enter.)* Elijah is focused again on following God's will, but the problem of King Ahab and Queen Jezebel is still very much alive.

(Ahab goes to one side and curls up on the floor. His back is to Jezebel as she walks up to him.)

JEZEBEL: *(loudly)* Ahab! What's wrong with you? Why aren't you up? Why aren't you eating?

AHAB: *(turning and sitting up to face Jezebel)* I'm so angry! I want to buy Naboth's vineyard so I can have a vegetable garden close to our palace. But he won't sell it to me! He says I can't have it! He said it has to stay in his family! *(Raises hands and slams them up and down like a spoiled child.)*

JEZEBEL: I don't believe this! Ahab, aren't you the King of Israel? Get up and eat! Leave it to me; I'll get that vineyard for you!

NARRATOR: Jezebel did get the vineyard from poor Naboth, her way. She frames Naboth in a lie, and he is accused of cursing God and the King. He is stoned to death as punishment. Now, King Ahab could have his vegetable garden.

(Jezebel helps Ahab stand and they hug. Jezebel leaves the stage and Ahab walks to the front where Elijah and Elisha are entering.)

KING AHAB: *(to Elijah)* so, you found me, enemy!

ELIJAH: The Lord God says, "You murdered Naboth for his property. On the same spot that dogs saw Naboth die, they will watch you die!" *(King Ahab starts to pull at his clothes in anguish.)* "As for Jezebel, she will die a horrible death! In fact, your whole family will be wiped out because you've made God so angry and caused others to sin."

(Ahab crawls around the stage making sobbing noises to punctuate the narration.

NARRATOR: In the years ahead, Ahab is killed in battle, and when his body is returned to Samaria for burial, dogs are at the scene. *(Ahab leaves stage)* Later, Queen Jezebel is thrown out a window by some palace workers. No one seems to care, no one helps her and she dies.

(Elijah and Elisha walk together across the stage.)

ELIJAH: *(to Elisha)* The Lord wants me to go ahead. Stay here, Elisha.

ELISHA: No! I will not leave you. I'm going with you! *(They silently appear to argue as narrator reads.)*

NARRATOR: Three times Elijah told Elisha to wait, and three times Elisha refused. He would not be separated from Elijah. They traveled from Gilgal to Bethel, and on to Jericho. During this time prophets asked Elisha when God was going to take Elijah. Elisha knew, but he would not talk about it.

ELIJAH: Elisha, stay here. The Lord God wants me to go to the Jordan River.

ELISHA: Absolutely not! I will not leave you, Elijah!

NARRATOR: So the two walked on towards the Jordan River. *(Sign has been placed at stage side.)* Fifty prophets followed them in the distance. It is about 600 years since the famous parting of the Red Sea. Watch carefully!

(Elijah and Elisha walk towards the audience. In their "mind's eye," they stop and look at the "river" and Elijah removes his cloak. He rolls it up and strikes the "river" with it the cloak.

ELISHA: The river! It's parted so we can walk through!

ELIJAH: Let us go now, Elisha. *(Both walk a short distance, looking left and right at the "parted waters.")* We've made it to the other side! Now I have a question for you, Elisha. The Lord will soon take me away. What can I do for you before I go?

ELISHA: You can give me twice the power of your spirit.

ELIJAH: Hmm... That will be tough, but listen; if you see me when I am taken away, then you will receive your request.

NARRATOR: *(Lights dim)* Suddenly, a flaming chariot, pulled by flaming fiery horses, cuts between Elijah and Elisha. *(Pull wagon decorated with flames run onstage pulled by at least one person dressed as a "horse" goes between Elijah and Elisha, almost hitting them, visibly separating them.)*

(Loud wind is heard, lights dim, and a smoke/vapor effect that will shoot vapor up vertically from inside the chariot wagon.)

NARRATOR continues: There is a mighty wind, and Elijah is taken up into heaven in a whirlwind. Elisha sees this and cries out, "My father! My father! The chariots and horseman of Israel!" And with that, Elisha saw Elijah no more.

(Total darkness is possible now. Elijah drops his cloak and quickly disappears offstage with the chariot while spot light focuses only on the vapor/wind event onstage and Elisha. Elisha stands in awe, looks down and sees a cloak. He picks it up, and again looks skyward. Raise lights.)

NARRATOR continues: While Elijah stayed close to God his whole life, the people swayed back and forth between the Lord God and Baal. Elijah showed great obedience and faith when he listened to God and ran the fiery contest to force the people to make a choice. The people had to see the Lord God was their one and only God. Elijah was also very human. When he hid from Queen Jezebel and King Ahab, he was so terrified and discouraged that he wanted to die. Elijah knew he couldn't do it alone. His faith, knowing that God walked with him, is what strengthened him. It is Elijah we see in the future, almost 1,000 years from now on a mountain talking with Moses and Jesus! Finally, God knew that Elijah's heart was open to hearing God speak in a still, small voice. It is just this still, small voice that we must listen for as God directs us on our journey. At any time we may be told to obey with acts of faith as Elijah. Are you ready for God to set the fire?

THE END

ELISHA
I Kings 19, II Kings 1-7, 9

CAST (Grouped by measure of involvement in play, most to least)
** Double Parts...Actors can double up on these parts.

SPEAKING PARTS

Narrator: Adult - The narrator will read connecting explanations between dialogues.
Elisha: Adult male- He should have
Prophet #1: Older boy, girl, or adult**
Prophet #2: Older boy, girl, or adult**
Naaman: Older boy or adult
Naaman's Wife: Older girl or adult
Naaman's Girl Servant: Girl**
Naaman's Male Servant: Older boy or adult**
Widow: Older girl or adult**
Son #1: Boy, any age**
Son #2: Boy, any age**
Woman of Shunem: Older girl or adult**
King of Samaria: Older boy or adult**
King of Syria: Older boy or adult**
Officer of Syria: Older boy or adult**
Elisha's Servant (Gehazi): Older boy or adult**
Man of Jericho: Older boy or adult**
Soldiers of Syria: Any age**

NONSPEAKING PARTS

Extra Prophets: Three - any age**
Son of Woman of Shunem: Young boy**
Walker of pole moon(s): Any age- able to walk with pole**
Walker of pole star(s): Any age- able to walk with pole**
Children of Israel (kidnap victims): Three or more - any age**

STAGE

The scenes will be enacted on the same stage. Simple props will be noted before narration.
Scenes will flow together by association with the cast's dialogue and movement.

SETTING

The side wall of a house is placed at the rear of the stage area from the beginning. A pile of
rocks will support a sign reading "Spring Water." At the other side of the stage a sign will be
propped up reading "Jordan River." (The "Welcome to Samaria" sign will be placed later.)

PROPS

- Elijah's cloak of hair (possibly a fur coat)
- Jordan River sign
- Rocks to form a spring
- "Spring Water" sign
- "Welcome to Samaria, A Secure, Gated Community" sign
- Bowl (small)
- Salt (In a small bag)
- 5 small plastic jars (small enough to be carried by one person at the same time)
- 1 jar (full of enough liquid to fill the smaller 5)
- Baby doll
- Stack of towels (10 or more)
- King of Samaria's robe with tear-off pieces
- Staff
- 6 pairs of socks (worn simultaneously) that will easily be removed
- 2 crowns
- Sound effects of: 1) water splashing 2) oncoming horses or people
- Pole moon and stars
- Spotlight
- Basket that Naaman's servant offers Elisha

ELISHA - The Play Begins

NARRATOR: The great prophet, Elijah stayed close to God his whole life. He led the battle against the people's interest in the idol god, Baal. With a contest of fire, Elijah proved the Lord God was the one and only God. But being human, Elijah experienced weakness and as time passed, grew tired and afraid. God stayed with Elijah and when his work on earth was almost done, God told him the name of his replacement: Elisha. Elijah found Elisha working a farm for his parents. Once Elisha said goodbye to his parents he took his place beside the great prophet Elijah. Elisha did not leave Elijah's side. He was devoted to him. Other prophets followed them, watching for the day when Elijah would leave. That time came soon after Elijah parted the Jordan River by hitting it with his cloak, allowing them to walk across it on dry ground. The same day, Elisha asks Elijah for a double portion of the Spirit of God that had been given to Elijah. Elijah responded that what Elisha was requesting would be difficult at best. But, he said that if Elisha saw when Elijah would be "taken up" to the heavens, *then* Elisha would receive the double portion of the spirit. Otherwise, Elisha's request would not be granted.

(Lights dim to darkness. High wind sound effects are heard.)

NARRATOR continues: Soon after horses of fire cut between Elijah and Elisha with a chariot of fire, Elijah is taken up into heaven by a whirlwind. Elisha sees Elijah swept up. Next, he is stunned by what he finds at his feet when he looks down.

(Lights are turned up. Five prophets have entered and stand in the background pointing and murmuring.)

ELISHA: Look! Here is Elijah's cloak! It must have fallen when the chariot of fire and fiery horses separated us...or when he was taken up in the great swirling windstorm!

(Elisha picks up the cloak and carries it to the "Jordan River" which a sign indicates.)

ELISHA: Earlier, when we crossed the Jordan River Elijah hit the water and it parted so we could walk across. I wonder... *(Pauses and stares at the river)* Where, oh where, is the Lord God? Where is Elijah's great God?

(Elisha raises the cloak and hits the water with the cloak. He jumps back in shock.)

ELISHA: The Jordan! It has parted again, and this time, for me!

(The 5 prophets, who are following in the background, point and go "ooh and ah." Elisha gleefully prances through the Jordan to the other side.)

PROPHET #1: The Spirit of the great Prophet Elijah is now with Elisha!

(As Elisha slips Elijah's cloak over his own shoulders, the prophets approach.)

PROHPET #2: Elisha, let our servants go and look for Elijah.

ELISHA: No, don't send them.

PROPHET #1: But what if Elijah's out there waiting? We should at least try.
(Elisha and prophets stare at each other as if in a standoff.)

NARRATOR: When Elisha saw the determination in their eyes, he agreed so their worry could be put to rest. They searched, and Elisha was proven right. Elijah was not to be found. (*5 prophets walk to side and freeze.)* From this time, about 848 B.C., God performed many miracles through the prophet Elisha. One day, when Elisha was living in Jericho, a man of the city came to him with a serious water pollution problem.

MAN of JERICHO: Elisha, our town's water is bad. Nothing will grow in the soil without good water. We can't figure out what the problem is. The town is built in the right place. What do you think?

ELISHA: Bring me a new bowl. Put some salt in the bowl before you bring it to me.

(Man of Jericho rushes off to take bowl and salt from stagehand and returns to hand it to Elisha.)

ELISHA: Come to the water spring with me.

(Elisha and man of Jericho walk over to a pile of rocks with the sign, "Spring Water.")

ELISHA: (*Gently moves man aside and tosses the salt toward the spring as he speaks)* The Lord God says, "I have healed this water. It will never again cause death. It will not stop anything from growing on the land."

(Man of Jericho waves his hands with joy and runs off the stage. Elisha freezes in place.)

NARRATOR: This was Elisha's first miracle. He was sure to point out that the Lord God had healed the water so the people are reminded that God is still with them, helping them, despite their stubborn disobedience.

(The five prophets come forward to the corner opposite Elisha to face the audience. Prophets #1and #2 speak to each other and turn to face the audience as if the audience members are listening prophets.)

PROPHET #1: Elisha sure is different from good old Elijah!

PROPHET #2: What do you mean? He's already parted the Jordan River. And he's doing wonderful miracles!

PROPHET #1: Don't you see? Elisha is more mild mannered with the people. Elijah was so bold. He was like the whirlwind that took him away!

PROPHET #2: You're right. They dress differently, too. Elijah always looked like he belonged in the wilderness, especially with that cloak of camel's hair. It makes me wonder how Elijah could have passed that cloak down to Elisha.

PROPHET #1: Yep! They're two very different people who have the same message from God. Our Lord God must know what he's doing!

(All prophets leave stage. Elisha stands and stretches where he has been frozen. The widow walks onstage and runs over to him.)

WIDOW: Elisha! My husband is dead. You remember him; he was one of your servants!

ELISHA: Yes, tell me how I can help.

WIDOW: My husband owes money to a man, and I cannot pay the debt! He is coming to take my two sons away to work as his slaves! You must help me, Elisha!

ELISHA: Tell me, woman, and what do you have in your house?

WIDOW: Just a little oil. We have nothing else. *(Widow stands facing Elisha, clenched hands up to her face, visibly trembling as she listens to Elisha.)*

ELISHA: Go to your neighbors and collect as many empty jars as you can. Then take them inside your house with your sons and shut the door. Next, pour the oil you do have into all the jars. As each of the jars is filled, put it aside.

(Elisha freezes in place. Widow releases her hands, spreads her fingers wide and raises her hands as if in despair as she runs from the stage and into the audience. She speaks to individuals in the audience while simultaneously peaking under chairs to suggest bottles may be found there. Her two sons quietly enter the stage and stand in front of house wall while she is in the audience. The largest jar, which has enough liquid to fill the 5 smaller jars, is placed on the floor next to them.)

WIDOW: Oh dear neighbor. I am in need of empty jars. Do you have any I could use?

(Widow goes to areas in the audience where she knows jars have been placed in order to collect the five that have been hidden. Once she has the five she returns to the stage where her sons jump up and down and clap their hands with joy when they see her.)

WIDOW: Sons! Bring the little oil we have over here. *(She gently lays the bottles on the ground.)* Be careful! *(One son picks the large jar up off floor where he and his brother have been standing.)*

WIDOW: Both of you- help me watch so I don't over fill these jars. We must not waste any precious oil! It is all that we have.

SON #1: *(Jar #1 is filled)* O.K., Mother. That's enough.

WIDOW: Put the filled jars over by the window as we finish with each one. And when you're over there look out and see if you see anyone coming! *(Son #1 does so and looks out the window.)*

SON #2: *(Jar #2 is filled)* Oops! I have to wipe a little off the top.
(Does so, takes it to side, and acts as if he looks out window.)

SON #1: *(Jar #3 is filled)* A little more... where is it coming from, Mother?

WIDOW: Don't ask questions! Just do as I say!
(Son #1 places Jar #3 with the others, and looks out the window again.)

SON #2: *(Jar #4 is filled)* I don't get it! Slower, a little more...there, stop!
(Son #2 places Jar #4, and again checks the window.)

WIDOW: Let's fill the last jar quickly.

SON #1: *(holds up jar and shakes his head while the widow pours)* I just don't understand. Where is this good oil coming from? Almost...O.K. Stop! *(He rushes it over to the others and puts the last jar down. Both sons walk over to the widow who is now holding the jug over her palm as if to pour it. They see nothing come out. They look at each other in amazement.)*

WIDOW: It's empty! Now that we've run out of containers, the oil is gone! Sons, stay here with the oil. I'll be right back! *(She runs over to where she left Elisha earlier.)*

WIDOW: Elisha! Elisha! I did as you said, and our jars are filled with oil! Then the oil stopped as soon as we ran out of jars to contain it!

ELISHA: Take the oil you now have, and sell it. Use the money to pay your dead husband's debts. Live on the rest of the money with your sons.

(Widow prayerfully bows and runs back to hers sons; all leave stage. Elisha slowly paces back and forth. His servant, Gehazi, quietly joins him on stage.

NARRATOR: Elisha was often on the road. In some towns, like Shunem, people let him stay in their homes when he was passing through. A wealthy couple in Shunem kept a room available in their house for Elisha to use when he was in town. One day Elisha asked the woman of the house a question.

(Woman of Shunem walks onstage and goes over to Elisha. Her servant follows behind her.)

ELISHA: Woman, you have been so kind to me by allowing me to stay in your home. How can I re-pay you?

WOMAN of SHUNEM: Oh, don't worry about it, Elisha. I'm fine!

GEHAZI (Elisha's servant): *(to Elisha)* There is one thing...She has no child and her husband is old.

ELISHA: Then, woman, about this time next year you will hold a son in your arms! *(Elisha freezes in place.)*

WOMAN of SHUNEM: No, don't say something that will not happen.
(She quickly leaves stage)

NARRATOR: *(Speaks as woman of Shunem returns to walk across and again off stage as she cradles an imaginary baby in her arms.)* The Woman of Shunem does have a son, and everything is fine until one day. One day the son becomes ill... and dies!

WOMAN of SHUNEM: *(returning to stage by herself, she looks confused, and calls out as she looks all around)* Elisha! I must find Elisha! Oh where is the man of God? Elisha! *(She is greatly upset and running around the stage.)*

NARRATOR: The woman eventually finds Elisha on Mount Carmel.

WOMAN of SHUNEM: *(Runs up to where Elisha is sitting still, and she falls at his feet.)* Oh, Elisha, my son is dead! *(She sobs)*

ELISHA: *(Turns to his servant, Gehazi, and hands him his staff.)* Go and run ahead with my staff. Stop for no one. When you reach the boy lay the staff on his face.

(Servant runs off in a circle around the stage and Elisha and woman follow. The woman Is crying loudly. The servant stops at the house wall which is at the rear of the stage area. The servant appears to go inside it by walking behind it. Just as Elisha and the woman reach the house wall the servant comes out. At this time Prophet #1 and #2 join them on stage as onlookers.)

SERVANT (GEHAZI): Elisha, the boy has not awakened! *(Servant walks over to comfort the woman while Elisha walks inside - behind the wall. Suddenly, seven loud sneezes are heard from inside the house. Elisha comes to the front of the house with the boy who is rubbing his nose.)*

ELISHA: Woman, take your son!

(The boy and mother hug each other and leave stage. Elisha sits down by the wall looking tired. The servant goes to wait behind the house wall. The two prophets walk to the front of the stage.)

PROPHET #1: Wasn't that interesting! But you know, I'm surprised food wasn't used in that miracle! Have you noticed how Elisha seems to have a knack with food?

PROPHET #2: No, what do you mean?

PROPHET #1: Oh, weren't you at Gilgal?

PROPHET #2: No. You know how there's not enough time now for all we prophets have to do!

PROPHET #1: You're right! Well, Elisha was holding a meeting with other prophets. It was time to eat. You know how hungry all that talking makes us! Elisha told his servants to make a big pot of stew.

PROPHET #2: Right, my stomach is grumbling already! What was in it?

PROPHET #1: That's where the stomachs more than grumbled. They turned sour! One of the servants had found a wild vine in the field. He cut it up along with herbs and other gourds. He mixed them all together in the pot.

PROPHET #2: So what went wrong?

PROPHET #1: As soon as we began to eat we knew it was bad. Different men started screaming there was death in the pot. Then we all put down our spoons!

PROPHET #2: What did Elisha do?

PROPHET #1: It was amazing. The man of God just said, "Get some flour." Then Elisha added it to the pot. Then he said to serve it again!

PROPHET #2: And did they eat it?

PROPHET #1: Every last bite! It was delicious!

PROPHET #2: Here's another food story. Did you hear about how Elisha and the Lord God fed 100 with just 20 loaves of bread?

PROPHET #1: What did he throw in this time? Once he used salt to clean the water, then he used flour to make the stew edible. How about sugar?

PROPHET #2: Oh, even better than sugar and better even than gold! Elisha added the Lord God's words. He told his servants what God's words were, and I quote, "Give it to the people; they'll even have some left over!"

PROPHET #1: Elisha truly is a man of God and a man of many wonderful miracles!

(Both prophets walk off the stage. Soldiers of Syria come onstage from one side and Children of Israel from the other. The soldiers chase the Israelites, capturing them, and round them up on the stage. This continues during narrator's reading.)

NARRATOR: When Solomon died the lands of the Children of Israel split into two separate kingdoms. The Southern Kingdom was called Judah. The Northern Kingdom was called Israel and was under frequent attacks by neighboring Syrians. It was made worse by the Syrians kidnapping the children of Israel and taking them captive inside their own country. One of the captives was a little girl who became a slave in the house of Naaman, a Syrian army commander. Naaman was very ill with leprosy, a skin disease.

(The soldiers drag the kidnap victims off the stage. Naaman and his wife walk on stage. Naaman has trouble walking. The girl slave-servant follows behind carrying a stack of towels. Across the stage, by the Jordan River, Naaman and his wife stop; Naaman sits down and holds his feet. His wife and the girl servant wrap the towels around his feet and try to make him comfortable. The stack of towels is left there.)

NAAMAN'S WIFE: *(to girl servant)* I am very worried, little one. My husband is so sick with leprosy. There is nothing I can do to help him.

NAAMAN'S GIRL SERVANT: If only he could see the prophet who is in my country, in Samaria. He is a man of God. He can cure my master!

NARRATOR: Arrangements are made, and Naaman is allowed to enter enemy territory of Samaria in the Northern Kingdom to seek help from Elisha.

(Elisha walks from where he has been sitting against the house wall and meets Naaman who is hobbling toward him. He is assisted by his male servant.)

ELISHA'S SERVANT: I am Elisha's messenger.

NAAMAN: What should I do, oh man of God? What can I do to cure myself of leprosy?

ELISHA'S SERVANT: Go and wash yourself seven times in the Jordan River. Your flesh will be restored, and you will be cleansed. *(Elisha sits on ground.)*

(Naaman throws up his hands, clenches his fists, and turns to hobble away. He angrily speaks to servant who is helping him.)

NAAMAN: Is that all he can say? Why aren't the rivers in my country as good as rivers here?

NAAMAN'S MALE SERVANT: But sir, if the prophet told you to do some super duper thing, wouldn't you have just gone and done it? Why not just try what he says?

(Naaman looks at the servant for a moment, nods, and turns to head back for where the Jordan River sign is. He sits down and motions as if he is bathing. He stands, dries himself - with the towels still there - and sits down again to bathe. He repeats this seven times. Each time he dries his feet, he removes a pair of socks (7 pairs that are meant to be skin, are on at once to give the appearance that he is shedding the old skin and that he is seeing healing with each washing / drying of his feet. Naaman counts each bath out loud.)

NAAMAN: One- two- three- four- five- six-seven...I am cured! *(Naaman holds out hands and feet as servant claps his hands. Both return to where Elisha is seated.)*

NAAMAN: *(To Elisha excitedly)* Oh man of God! Now I know that there is truly only one God, and He is the God of Israel! Please accept my gifts. *(Naaman holds out basket as servant hands them to him.)*

ELISHA: As positive as I am of God's life, I am positive I will take nothing for God's work.

NAAMAN: O.K., but may the Lord God forgive me in the future when it may appear that I am bowing down to the other gods my people worship. I, myself, bow down to the only God, the true God.

ELISHA: Go in peace. *(Elisha joins his servant behind the house wall. Naaman leaves the stage. Soldiers of Syria enter and without any sound, pretend to fight. The King of Syria enters and watches them silently while narrator reads.)*

NARRATOR: Despite the good will between Elisha, who lived in the Kingdom of Israel, and Naaman, who lived on the enemy's side, Naaman's king continued to attack Israel. One day the King of Syria began to wonder why the Israelites seemed to always be one step ahead of his own army. He thought one of his men was leaking information.

KING of SYRIA: Who's leaking our secrets? Who is the spy from our side who is helping the King of Israel know what we're planning to do?

OFFICER of SYRIA: It's Elisha, the prophet on their side. It's not one of our men! Elisha repeats your exact words to his king, the King of Samaria.

KING of SYRIA: *(Stomping his foot in anger.)* Bring Elisha to me! Find Elisha! I want him here!

(Lights dim to indicate night. The "Welcome to Samaria- A Secure and Gated Community" sign is placed. Stars and a moon may be carried out to show the night timing. A light is beamed on the house wall. Elisha and his servant come out. A rumble of horses and noise is heard getting louder and louder. King of Syria and officers leave stage.)

SERVANT (GEHAZI) *(Turning quickly and looking around and pointing in all directions.)* Elisha! We are surrounded! What shall we do?

ELISHA: *(Calmly)* Don't be afraid. There are more on our side than on their side. *(Elisha turns and bows to pray while servant- Gehazi walks off a bit with his hands on his head in worry)* Oh Lord! Open his eyes so that he may see!"

SERVANT (GEHAZI): *(Suddenly)* Oh! I see them! I see what you're talking about!

(Syrian soldiers come on stage from opposite side of where the Servant Gehazi is looking. They walk towards Elijah and enact a slow motion towards him as he prays.)

ELISHA: Oh Lord, I hear the enemy approach. Strike these people with blindness!

(The approaching soldiers suddenly grab their faces and bump into each other and fall to their knees screaming in fear.)

ELISHA: *(to servant, Gehazi)* Follow me! We're going to talk to the enemy!
(Elisha and servant walk up to the blinded soldiers.)
If you are looking for Elisha, you're going the wrong way. Follow me, and I will lead you to him!

(Elisha leads the stumbling soldiers to the front of the stage where a sign reads, "Welcome to Samaria- A Secure, Gated Community.")

ELISHA: *(Speaks to soldiers.)* Stop here. *(He lifts his arms and face in prayer)*
Lord, now that the enemy is secure within the city of Samaria, open their eyes so they can see!

(Soldiers rub eyes and start screaming)

SOLDIERS: Oh no! We've been tricked!

KING of SAMARIA: *(Walks on the stage and over to Elisha)*
Oh, man of God! Should I kill them? Should I kill the enemy you have brought within my walls?

ELISHA: No, they're already beaten down enough. Give them...hmmm, give them food, and then send them home.

NARRATOR: Once again, Elisha cooks up a tasteful ending to a miracle. But there is still a bitter truth about the people's deeds that God cannot "stomach." Despite the success of the great fire contest led by Elijah to prove the One, true God... the idol god, Baal, is still worshiped by many of the people. Elisha picks up where Elijah left off, as a prophet and follows God's directions. Elisha anoints Jehu as the new king of the Kingdom of Israel. God wants Jehu to complete the earlier promise made through Elijah, to wipe out the evil Baal-worshipping house of King Ahab and his priests. This is done, yet it is not enough to turn all the people around to God Almighty. But God has not given up. More prophets are on the way, but for how long? What will make the Children of Israel listen?

THE END

JONAH
Jonah 1- 4

CAST (Grouped by measure of involvement in play, most to least)
**Actors can double up on these parts.*

SPEAKING PARTS

Narrator #1: Adult
Narrator #2: Adult
Jonah: Older student or adult. Jonah needs a strong voice and a convincing angry pout.
God's Voice: Older student or adult with good balance
Boat Captain: Older student or adult with good balance**
Sailors: At least 2, any age, with good balance**
Ninevite #1: Any age **
Ninevite #2: Any age**
Ninevite #3: Any age**
Ninevite #4: Any age**

NONSPEAKING PARTS

Boat operators: Older students or adults for behind the scenes physical work**
Whale operators: Older students or adults for behind the scenes physical work**
Ninevites: As many as possible, any age**
Moon pole carrier: Any age**
Star pole carrier: Any age**
Sun pole carrier: Any age**
Worm: Any age, must make loud chomping sounds**
Boat mover: Any age**
Fish mover: Any age**

STAGE

The scenes will be enacted on the same stage. Simple props will be noted before narration.
Scenes will flow together by association with the casts' dialogue and movement. Narration will
be done by two people to give the feeling of God's being all knowing and present and all times.

SETTING

A lightweight material boat side with braces for sliding on the back is placed at the far side of
the stage. Boat operators will rock it to varying degrees. The large fish is constructed the same
way and appears on the other side of the stage. Sturdy step stools behind each will enable
actors to appear as if in or on the set. A mural of the city of Nineveh is in the background. Light
will shine on this once Jonah goes there.

PROPS

- Mural backdrop of Nineveh
- "40 days left" sign
- 2 pieces of heavy cardboard that can fit together to form a makeshift "A frame"
- Boat image made of heavy cardboard
- Coin (for coin toss on the boat)
- Cardboard painted boxes to look like crates
- Fans and dust.
- Green outfit for worm
- Large fish image of heavy cardboard
- Leafy grape leaf vine netting
- Light with wide beam to shine on mural
- Long teeth (maybe)
- Moon on pole
- Oars
- Star on pole
- Step stools to match the number of sailors and Jonah
- Sound effect of metal clinking on wood
- Sound effect of rooster crowing
- Sound effects of roaring, splashing waves in a storm
- Sun on pole

JONAH - The Play Begins

NARRATOR #1: Elisha is dead, and Israel, the Northern Kingdom, continues to fight off invaders. Over 600 years ago, the Israelites began their disobedience when they broke the covenant God made with them on Mount Sinai with Moses and the Ten Commandments. God wants them to remember that he was the one who freed them from the slavery of the Egyptians and that he is the one who has taken care of them throughout the centuries. But the people forget and fail to realize that it is the Lord God, alone, who loves them so much. They ignore His warnings and they worship other gods. Despite this, the Lord God refuses to give up on them. He sends prophets, like Elijah, to remind them of His love. So many people witness the fire contest between the Lord God and Baal, but it does not sway them. Elisha followed that sign of God's presence with miracles of kindness. Still, the people's eyes are not open. They are blind to the truth of the one true and only God and consequently continue to disobey. Now here's a twist in the ongoing story. It's the popular Prophet Jonah's turn to obey God. Jonah has been a prophet in Israel, the Northern Kingdom. But today, he is going to get a very difficult assignment from God. It will be very difficult for Jonah to obey *because God will send Jonah to the people of Nineveh...enemies of the Israelites!* Jonah will not be happy!

(Jonah is sitting by a tree in the middle of the stage. Right hand over his eyes, he appears to be looking in the distance.)

GOD'S VOICE: Jonah! *(Jonah jumps up and looks all around.)* Jonah, go to the great city of Nineveh. Warn the people that I know how wicked they are.

(Jonah points in the direction of God's voice then claps his hand over his mouth in shock.)

NARRATOR #2: This is shocking to Jonah because Nineveh is the capital city of Assyria, the greatly feared and hated enemy of Israel. Visitors to Assyria reported the Assyrians to be extremely cruel and ferocious.

(Jonah looks both ways and runs in the opposite direction of God's voice, of where he has just pointed.)

NARRATOR #1: Jonah is heading away from the voice!

NARRATOR #2: Jonah is running away from God!

NARRATOR #1: Jonah is disobeying the Lord God!

NARRATORS #1 and 2: Oh, no, Jonah! You're going the wrong way!

(Jonah reaches the boat at the stage side, walks behind, climbs a step stool behind it and is seen looking over with at least two sailors and the captain who are already on step stools. He appears to be giving them money for passage.)

NARRATOR #1: But Jonah does run. He runs to the sea where he boards a boat to escape from God and God's orders.

NARRATOR #2: Jonah must just be so afraid of the Ninevites that he's blinded to the truth that no one escapes from God!

(The sound effect of waves and a storm are heard. Boat operators begin to rock the boat with increasing intensity for about a minute. Actors on step stools move to give the effect they're being shaken up. Then, Jonah disappears from sight, off his stool.)

SAILOR #1: Oh, Captain! This storm looks like a bad one!

SAILOR #2: Start throwing crates off to lighten our load!

(Both start throwing empty boxes overboard.)

CAPTAIN: Where is our passenger... *(Boat lurches)* ... that Jonah character? Why isn't he up here... *(Boat lurches)* ... helping us?

SAILOR #1: He's down below deck, captain!

CAPTAIN: Get him up here, now! We must all pray... *(Boat lurches)* ... to our gods for help. Even I am scared, now!

SAILOR #2: *(Disappears then re-appears with Jonah who is rubbing his eyes)* Here he is, Captain. He was asleep!

CAPTAIN: Listen to... *(Boat lurches and all grab sides of boat)* Listen! We must pray to all the gods we have. You, Jonah.... pray to whoever your god is! Call him! Maybe he'll help us!

SAILOR #2: Let's toss a coin ... Let's see who got us into this trouble!

NARRATOR #1: Despite the storm they managed to toss a coin, *(sailors facing each other toss something and the sound of a loud "clink on wood" is heard)* and it was decided that...

NARRATOR #2: Jonah was the reason for the terrible storm!

(All turn to Jonah.)

CAPTAIN: So, Jonah... *(Ship lurches)* ...where are you from? What's the reason for this terrible storm?

JONAH: I am an Israelite. I worship the one true God, the God who created land... *(Boat lurches)* and sea! *(Boat lurches)*

SAILORS & CAPTAIN: *(All throw hands in air and scream in greater fear.)* Ooh!

NARRATOR #1: All are totally terrified now because they realize Jonah's God is after Jonah, and they are caught in the middle!

SAILOR #1: *(Calming down enough to talk)* So what did you do? What should we do to you...
(Boat lurches) ...to calm the waves?

JONAH: *(with some hesitation)* Throw me overboard! This is all my fault. Toss me into the sea.
Then it will calm down. *(Boat lurches.)*

CAPTAIN: Wait! Let's try the oars. *(Boat lurches as they pick up the oars from behind the ship.
It is now so rough that they appear to be stabbing the air, not water.)* It's no use! Drop the oars!
(They do so. Captain raises arms to sky) Oh, Lord! We have tried! Don't be angry with us for
throwing Jonah overboard!

*(The two sailors then pick Jonah up and toss him – gently - over the front of the boat. At the
same time the large fish is moved across from the other side of the stage, in enough time that
we do not see Jonah hit the "water." The fish then moves back so the boat can be seen again,
without Jonah, who is now behind the fish.)*

NARRATOR #1: The seas calmed down, and the boat was saved.
(Boat and related characters leave stage.)

NARRATOR#2: And so was Jonah. A great fish swallowed him! Jonah was alive inside the great
fish!

*(Fish is moved back and forth by behind the fish operators, across the stage 3 times each way to
represent 3 days and 3 nights.)*

NARRATOR #2: One day!

NARRATOR #1: One night!

NARRATOR #2: A second day!

NARRATOR #1: A second night!

NARRATOR #2: And a third day!

NARRATOR #1: And a third day!

*(Lights dim as the fish is turned around so that the other side, painted without fins, etc., is
backdrop for Jonah as he lies on his back with arms raised in prayer inside the fish. Fish
operators have moved to the other side. Light increases.)*

JONAH: Oh, Lord! I am so sorry! As I was thrown into the sea and was sinking deeper and
deeper, seaweed wrapped around me; but Lord, you saw me and sent this fish to save me by
swallowing me. I was wrong for running away from you. I know now that from the very
beginning I should have been obedient and followed your directions. O Lord, thank you for
saving me! I promise to obey you and I will do the job you gave me to do in the first place

NARRATOR: When Jonah realizes God sent the fish to save him he feels so grateful. He knows he must always obey God. Then, the Lord ordered the fish to free Jonah, *(Jonah jumps out of the mouth end of the fish and tumbles)* and he was vomited up onto dry land!

GOD'S VOICE: Jonah! *(Jonah comes out of his tumble and stands straight, looking towards God's voice with palms up as if to receive what God is about to tell him.)*

GOD'S VOICE continues: Jonah! Go to the city of Nineveh and tell the people the message I will give you.

(Light shines on city mural backdrop.)

JONAH: Yes, Lord, right away! *(As Jonah begins to walk back and forth across the stage, Ninevites – as many as possible – enter the stage and mill around Jonah. Some stop and stare, others walk past, stop and go back to him, a few walk past and ignore. All the time Jonah is calling out God's message.)*

Jonah cries out: "40 more days and Nineveh will be overthrown!" *(Jonah also carries the "40 days left" sign." After about 1 minute, all Ninevites stop in their tracks and turn to face Jonah. Then they turn to face the audience.)*

NINEVITE #1: We must fast! *(All cheer)*

NINEVITE #2: No more violence! *(All cheer)*

NINEVITE #3: Sack cloth for everyone! *(All cheer)*

NINEVITE #4: Maybe God will show compassion on us... *(All Ninevites break in.)*

ALL NINEVITES: Maybe we'll be saved! *(Loudest cheering of all. Then they become quiet and kneel. They raise their arms to God.)*

NARRATOR #1: And the Lord God DOES show compassion.

NARRATOR #2: After 40 days, God does not carry out the threatened destruction!

ALL NINEVITES: Praise the Lord God! Praise the Lord God! *(They continue but softer so Jonah can be heard.)*

(Jonah walks to the front of the stage between the Ninevites and audience and faces the audience. His hands are on his hips, and he looks angry. He looks up and speaks to God. At this time two pieces of heavy cardboard are slid out on the stage for later use as a makeshift "A frame" shelter.)

JONAH: Oh, Lord! I knew this would happen! I knew you'd let those Ninevites off the hook! That's why I didn't obey you the first time you told me to come here! *(Stomps his foot as he loudly exclaims)* Just let me die! *(Ninevites quietly leave Jonah alone on stage.)*

GOD'S VOICE: And just why, Jonah, do you think you should be angry?

(Jonah turns from the audience and stomps off to sit on down where he can keep an eye on the city of Nineveh mural. The sun on pole carrier comes on stage and holds the sun directly over Jonah's head. When Jonah first faces Nineveh he covers his eyes and acts as if he can't stand the glare.)

JONAH: Oh my eyes! The sun seems brighter today than usual!

(He then sits on the ground so the audience sees his profile; he can turn to view the city mural. Sun remains directly over his head.)

JONAH: What a hot day, and the sun is so bright. I'll use this old wood to make a makeshift covering from the sun. *(Jonah picks up two pieces of cardboard and balances them against each other as an A frame. He sits down under it and sticks his head out to see. The pole sun carrier quickly places a netting of grape leaves over the front of the frame where Jonah's head is. This may have been attached to the back of the sun. Jonah sticks head out further.)*

JONAH: Oh, where did that shade come from? Ah... *(Moves out in front of shelter and looks at Nineveh)* Now this is nice! What a difference a little vine can make! *(Head nods, then drops to his chest. Jonah snores.)*

NARRATOR #1: Night comes and Jonah rests from his stressful day. *(Jonah sleeps while sitting up. The lights dim. Pole held moon and stars may be carried out.)*

NARRATOR #2: But not everyone is asleep!
(Light shines on a worm, dressed in green, which crawls to the vine and starts gobbling making chomping sounds.) A certain worm is busy at work eating the vine that shades Jonah's head.

NARRATOR #1: It chews...

NARRATOR#2: And it chews... *(Worm removes green leaf netting and puts a brown rope to hang down in front of Jonah's face. Worm returns to ground and crawls off stage.)*

NARRATOR #1: The vine is completely withered and dry by the time Jonah wakes up!

(Lights brighten, sun on pole is carried out, rooster crows from backstage, and Jonah lifts his head off his chests. The sun on a pole is literally directly over his head. As he stretches his face bumps the rope vine that is left.)

JONAH: Oh! What is this? *(Startled)* My shade! My vine! Where did it go? What happened to it?

(A roaring sound of wind is heard whistling. Fans are turned on, and dust is blowing around in front to look like a windstorm.)

JONAH continues: Oh it is so hot already! And this wind is scorching! My shade is gone.... I wish I were dead!

GOD'S VOICE: Jonah! You are so concerned about this vine, this vine that lived just one day. You were so interested in this "thing" that you had nothing to do with at all. You did not plant it. You did not feed it or help it grow. You did not keep your eye on it every day and every night. Yet you are so wrapped up in the vine that when you lose it do you really think you have the right to be angry?

JONAH: *(Speaking with anger in his voice)* Yes, I do!

GOD'S VOICE: Angry enough to die?

JONAH: Yes! I am fed up! I am angry enough to die!

GOD'S VOICE: Alright, Jonah. Then chew on this! If you think you have the right to be angry about such a "one day vine," don't you think I, the Lord God, should be concerned about the city of Nineveh where 120,000 people can't tell their right hand from their left? Should I be any less concerned with people who I created and nurtured, than you are with a single vine?

NARRATOR #1: Jonah now sees God's point. The light of understanding dawns over Jonah as he realizes how kind and compassionate God is. He remembers how slow God is to anger, and how God always shows His love, even when we stop caring about ourselves or anything. He also remembers that no man, not even Jonah can save himself. It all depends on God's mercy, grace and love for all people.

NARRATOR #2: Wait! (*Worm runs across stage and off.*) What was that? Is that bad worm still here? What can this mean?

NARRATOR #1: So it is not gone. A worm is still alive in the city of Nineveh, despite the people's turning to the Lord God.

NARRATOR #2: While Jonah will be referred to hundreds of years from now by Jesus, can these days get any darker? Have God's mercy and forgiveness dried up like the grapevine? Will it grow back? Or is it that we are simply blind to it? Over a thousand years before, God held true to His promises starting with Abraham and has continued to speak through so many others over the centuries. God wants to use not only leaders, but ordinary men and women, to reach people today and tomorrow. God is not finished, and God certainly is not a quitter! If God calls on you today, which way will you turn?

THE END

DANIEL

Daniel 1-6

CAST (Grouped by measure of involvement in play, most to least.)
***Actors can double up on these parts.*

NOTE: While Shadrach, Meshach, and Abednego are included in this play, a separate play about them follows this one.

SPEAKING PARTS

Narrator: Adult
Daniel: Youthful, mature, elderly - may play all parts - there may be 3 actors for the different age levels of Daniel's life
King Nebuchadnezzar: Older boy**
Woman #1 at well: Older girl**
Woman #2 at well: Older girl**
King Belshazzar: Older boy
King Darius: Older boy
Shadrach: Older boy
Meshach: Older boy
Abednego: Older boy
Wise Man Speaker: Older boy**
Guard: Any age**
Official: Any age**
Man: Any age**
Persian #1: Any age**
Persian #2: Any age
Worker: Any age**
2 Servants: Any age**

NONSPEAKING PARTS

Walking light Bulb: Any age**
Guards: (2-3) Any age**
3-4 Trainees: Older boys**
3-4 Wise men: Any age boy**
4-5 Party goers: Any age** (rowdy)
6 Extras: Any age

STAGE

All scenes are done on a central stage area.

SETTING

A backdrop mural shows dry mountains in the distance. A well is made of rocks piled in a circle on stage. A later scene will show a palace wall (which could be a sheet with lines drawn to represent big blocks) on which a hand and words will be projected using an overhead projector.

ADDITIONAL PROPS

- 2 buckets
- Flutes and harps
- Gold neck chain
- Lamp stand
- Large cardboard lion's den with a step ladder on the inside and outside
- Overhead projector
- Purple robe
- Several gold and silver cups (could be covered with gold and aluminum foil)
- Sound Effects: 1) Battle 2) Roaring lion
- Throne chair
- Transparency and pen for wall writing
- Trumpet sound effects
- Walking light bulb costume

NOTE: If lighting cannot be controlled, stagehands can quickly move backgrounds and props on and off the stage.

DANIEL - The Play Begins

NARRATOR: Life goes on much as it had for the Children of Israel before the exile from Judah. The main difference is they are forced to live away from the Promised Land as exiles in Babylon in a land of pagan people.

(Two women are seen at well dipping buckets in for water. They recognize each other. Each puts down her bucket, and begins to talk.)

WOMAN #1: Oh! How are you, sister? How is your family? *(Extends arms and they hug)* I haven't seen you since our long walk here from Jerusalem.

WOMAN#2: I am fine. My husband and sons do the same work in Babylon as they did in Jerusalem. So we're slowly getting used to it.

WOMAN #1: My husband is one of the builders down by the Chebar River. They're digging a canal. It's hard work, but he's getting used to it, too.

WOMAN #2: By the river- *(hand to chin as if trying to remember)* isn't that where that worker, who is called the prophet Ezekiel, had an experience with God?

WOMAN #1: Why yes! My husband heard him speak. *(Pauses and says name carefully)* Then Ezekiel suddenly fell down flat and stared up at the sky!

WOMAN #2: And didn't he act very strange for the next few days?

WOMAN #1: That's what I heard! When he came to his senses he told a wild story about some vision of God! Do you believe--

WOMAN #2: Wait, what was the vision?

WOMAN #1: Ezekiel said he saw God in all His glory. God told Ezekiel to stand up and listen.

WOMAN #2: I bet he didn't argue.

WOMAN #1: He didn't have time. God's Spirit took control of Ezekiel and lifted him up. Then God told Ezekiel that he was sending him to preach his message to the stubborn people of Israel, whether they listened or not. God told Ezekiel not to be afraid.

WOMAN #2: Why bother then?

WOMAN #1: God said they would at least know he had sent a prophet to speak to them. Then God held out a scroll to him and told Ezekiel to eat it!

WOMAN #2: Eat it! *(Laughs)* Like this? *(Pantomimes eating with big gestures. Both women laugh.)*

WOMAN #1: Ezekiel said he obeyed God and ate it. Guess what he said it tasted like?

WOMAN #2: Oh this will be good... Hmm... Let's see; it would be flat, dry, and probably tasteless.

WOMAN #1: According to Ezekiel the scroll tasted like honey! But before Ezekiel ate it he saw what God had written on the scroll. They were words of sadness mourning and grief. After he ate the scroll it took him about a week to recover and to literally get back on his feet!

WOMAN #2: Well that would throw me off, too!

WOMAN #1: Now Ezekiel says he has to spend the rest of his life telling people about this. He's going all over Babylon preaching to our people of God's greatness and promise to return us to our homeland. He also says God will hold us responsible for our behavior.

WOMAN #2: Ezekiel reminds me of Jeremiah. Do you remember him in Jerusalem?

WOMAN #1: Who didn't hear of Jeremiah? What a troublemaker!

WOMAN #2: Yes, he did challenge people with his words. I remember him saying Nebuchadnezzar and the Babylonians would conquer us.

WOMAN #1: I remember the argument. We thought God would protect us because He was there in His temple.

WOMAN #2: And Jeremiah said we didn't deserve God's help!

WOMAN #1: He really was on our backs about following God's laws and making sacrifices the right way.

WOMAN #1: *(Pauses)* Jeremiah really didn't understand us and why we chose to do things our own way *(Both are silent for a few seconds.)*

WOMAN #2: Then again--

WOMAN #1: Maybe he did...

WOMAN #2: I remember he even got tossed into prison because he wouldn't stop prophesying and scaring the people with his words from God.

WOMAN #1: Jeremiah just refused to quit! I hear he's living in Egypt now. He's changed his story; now he says God will keep us in bondage until Babylon falls in 70 years. Then, after that, we will again be free from bondage! We will honor God, and we will be forgiven.

WOMAN #2: Do you think we should believe him?

WOMAN #1: Ah... just think free... forgiven! Let's pray that he is right!
(Both hug and step back to speak)

WOMAN #2: I'm so glad we ran into each other! Oh! *(Looking down)* We'd better not forget what we came here for! *(Points to buckets. Both laugh and pick up buckets and leave stage waving to each other.)*

(Shadrach, Meshach, Abednego and Daniel enter with a guard and 3-4 trainees following behind them. They are talking quietly to each other. All stop at the well the women have just left.)

GUARD: *(To Shadrach, Meshach, Abednego, and Daniel who are in the lead.)*
I still find it hard to believe. You ate nothing but vegetables and water for ten days when you could have had food from the King's table like the other trainees. *(Points to the trainees.)* Yet you ended up in better condition than all the rest. You four are all stronger *and* smarter, especially you, Daniel! King Nebuchadnezzar is surely pleased. You boys have a bright future here in Babylon.

DANIEL: Oh, but if only we were enjoying this success at home. We will always remember our God and the land he gave our ancestors before we were brought to this land.

SHADRACH, MESHACH, and ABEDNEGO: *(unison)* We'll praise our God forever!

DANIEL: We'll stick together on this, won't we guys?

(The four do high fives and march back and forth in drill formation while the narrator reads.)

NARRATOR: Shadrach, Meshach, Abednego, and Daniel impressed King Nebuchadnezzar, but Daniel impressed him the most. God made Daniel physically and mentally strong. Besides Daniel's physical strength and obvious intelligence, he was also very gifted at explaining the meaning of dreams, so he was also considered to be a "wise man." One day King Nebuchadnezzar called his wise men together (but not Daniel) because he was having upsetting dreams that he couldn't understand.

(Stage lights go off while Shadrach, Meshach, Abednego, and Daniel leave the stage. Well rocks and desert backdrop are removed to leave a blank background. King's throne is moved onto the stage and lights go on as King Nebuchadnezzar and several wise men walk on stage. The King sits upon his throne and the wise men line up in front of him.)

KING: Wise men! Listen to me carefully. I have been having a dream that I do not understand, and it is really beginning to bother me. I want to know its meaning.

WISE MAN SPEAKER: Your Majesty, we are here to help you. Just tell us what the dream was.

KING: No. *(Scans them slowly)* No. Not this time! I have decided that you will tell me the dream as well as its meaning.

(All wise men gasp and look at each other in disbelief)

KING: And if you do not do this, your punishment will be death!

(Each wise man grabs at his throat and looks terrified.)

NARRATOR: Of course, not one of the wise men could answer the king.

WISE MAN SPEAKER: But Your Highness, if you could just tell us the dream!

KING: *(Interrupting speaker, King yells)* No! Listen, wise men, *("wise" is said sarcastically)* **let me repeat,** if you don't tell me what my dream was about, plus give me the meaning, you will be killed and your homes will be ruined.

WISE MAN SPEAKER: But great King- *(The King turns quickly towards speaker and glares at him)* King Nebuchadnezzar, no man can tell you what was going on in your mind last night! Only heaven knows.

KING: Well then, I have news for you. You will die, as will all the other wise men in my kingdom! *(Waves arm towards wise men)* Guards! Take them away!
(King folds arms, looks down and becomes motionless.)

(Two guards enter and lead the wise men offstage where they meet Daniel coming in. Guard puts hand up to stop the wise men as he speaks to Daniel.)

GUARD: Daniel! Since you are a wise man because you also interpret dreams, I must take you with me. The King says *all* wise men must die!

DANIEL: *(shocked)* What has happened? What's the King's problem that these *(points to wise men)* wise men couldn't solve?

GUARD: This time the King did not tell them the details of his dream. He wanted THEM to tell HIM his bad dream as well as what it meant!

DANIEL: What? Oh no... Please take me to King Nebuchadnezzar. I'd like to speak with him.

(Guard looks at the whimpering wise men, then back at Daniel.)

GUARD: All right. You go ahead with this guard. I have to keep going with this group.
(Guard gently pushes the wise men offstage and Daniel and the other guard walk over to where the King sits.)

DANIEL: *(Walking up to the King as he comes to life again, Daniel bows, then slowly and strongly speaks.)* King Nebuchadnezzar, Your Highness, I have learned of your challenge to the wise men. Let me try to help you. Just give me a little time so I can talk to my God.

KING: Daniel, why should I give you time?

DANIEL: My hope is if I have time to talk to my God He will tell me your dream, for only He knows what was going on in your mind last night. Also King Nebuchadnezzar, please hold the order to have all the wise men killed.

KING: Well, Daniel, for you... all right! Go now and come back with the answers!
(Guard and Daniel walk away from King. Shadrach, Meshach, and Abednego walk on stage towards Daniel.)

DANIEL: My friends! Please pray that God tells me the King's dream and explains it to me. Otherwise, all wise men will die!

(King puts hands in lap and looks down and freezes. The three friends huddle around Daniel as the guard walks to the side of the stage and freezes. Daniel goes to one side where he kneels to pray. His friends go to the other side and do the same. Lights dim to indicate night as the narrator speaks.)

NARRATOR: That night Daniel prayed and prayed to his God. *(Light bulb walks across behind Daniel who moves as if startled.)* God answered Daniel. He showed the dream and its meaning to him.

(Shadrach, Meshach, Abednego leave stage as lights come on and Daniel stretches and stands.)

DANIEL: Oh, God! I will praise you forever! You know everything. You control human events. You explain mysteries. I thank you for telling me the King's dream and its meaning!
(Daniel walks confidently over to where seated King becomes animated again.)

KING: Well, Daniel, do you know the dream and its meaning?

DANIEL: Oh King Nebuchadnezzar, no human could answer that question. Only God can do those things, and He showed them to me as I prayed. Through your dream God wants to show you what will happen in your kingdom in the future!

KING: *(leaning forward)* Yes, Daniel. Go on.

DANIEL: But Your Highness, you must understand that I was given the meaning ONLY so you would understand the dream. I am no smarter than anyone else is.

KING: The dream, Daniel! The dream!

DANIEL: Your Majesty, in your dream a frightening, giant statue stood in front of you. It was very shiny. The head was gold. The chest and arms were silver. It was bronze from the waist to the knees, and iron from the knees to the ankles. At the base the feet were a mix of iron and clay.

KING: Yes! Yes! You are correct! Now tell me what it all means!

DANIEL: Let's start at the top. The head of gold stands for you. God has made you ruler over all. A weaker kingdom will replace you. The kingdom of bronze will replace that kingdom. It will rule the whole world. After that a king of iron will crush everything. The fourth kingdom will be both strong and weak; that's why you see the clay and iron mixture. That kingdom will crumble because iron and clay don't mix. You also saw a stone being cut from a mountain that fell and hit the feet, shattering both. King Nebuchadnezzar, you can believe all of this because my great God told me it would happen! Believe it!

KING: *(Stands and bows to Daniel)* I know now that your God is greater than all other gods and kings because he gave you the answer.

(King and Daniel leave the stage so that no one is left on the stage.)

(Stage lights go off as the narrator speaks. King's throne is removed and stage lights go on.)

NARRATOR: The King honored Daniel with gifts and promoted him to be a governor and head wise man. Daniel remembered his friends who had helped him pray, and at his request, the King also promoted them. Daniel was very loyal to his King, his friends, and most of all to his God.

(Worker enters carrying a large statue. The official, the King, Person #1 and 6 extras follow him.)

NARRATOR: Years passed. One day King Nebuchadnezzar ordered a huge statue to be set up near Babylon. *(Group stops and worker sets up statue.)*

MAN: *(staring at statue)* Wow! How big is that thing?

WORKER: It's 90 feet high and 9 feet wide. And you'd better not call it a "thing". The King ordered it to be built and put here.

OFFICIAL: All of you: Pay attention! I have a new command from the King. Soon you will hear all kinds of musical instruments play. You'll hear trumpets, flutes, and harps. From now on, whenever you hear the music the King orders you to bow down and to worship this statue. If you do not... *(He turns and scans the audience.)* If you do not, you will be thrown into the fiery furnace!

(All cower. Music is heard, and all bow down. Simultaneously, Shadrach, Meshach, and Abednego enter stage, walk by, and merely glance at the statue. The official sees them and chases after them as the narrator speaks. Everyone leaves stage and stage lights go off. Statue is removed from stage and white backdrop is put up for future wall writing. King's throne is put on stage with purple robe, gold chain in bag behind throne.)

NARRATOR: To make a long story short, because Shadrach, Meshach and Abednego refused to bow to anyone or anything other than their God, they were thrown into the fire burning furnace. God not only gave them courage to stand up for their beliefs, He walked in the fire with them! The King himself witnessed how the men were protected in the fire when he looked in the furnace and saw an angelic looking being walking with the three in the midst of the blazing fire. The King shouted for the men to come out of the fire, He quickly realized that the fire had not harmed their bodies, their hair or their robes, plus, there was no smell of fire on them! Once again, just like he had acknowledged Daniel's God after the dream explanation, King Nebuchadnezzar again bowed to the God of Daniel and the captive Israelites.

Once again the exiled people were given encouragement to hold on, to believe in their God and His ultimate promise. God had not left them alone in exile. God was in control and all Babylonians saw it!

(Stage lights go on. A white haired and physically aged Daniel slowly walks across the stage with a cane. He stands silently surveying the audience as the narrator continues.)

NARRATOR: Years pass. Daniel is now over 70 years old.

DANIEL: *(addresses audience)* King Nebuchadnezzar is dead. As I predicted from the King's dream, a weaker ruler would replace him. That ruler is his son. Why, here comes King Belshazzar now.

(Points ahead as King Belshazzar walks from the rear of the audience appearing to be slightly drunk. He casually carries a cup upside down as he makes his way forward to Daniel.)

DANIEL: He doesn't appear to be too worried that our strong and power hungry neighbors, the Persians, are at our doorstep!

DANIEL continues: *(to Belshazzar who Is slightly unbalanced but not totally out of control.)* Hello Belshazzar! I hear you are preparing for another big party!

BELSHAZZAR: I sure am! This time I'm having a thousand of my top officials over to party, party, party! I'm sure you'll hear all about it!
(Stumbles off to side of stage where he greets arriving partygoers who are loud and rowdy as they all enter the stage.)

DANIEL: *(Glancing over at rowdy partygoers)* I'm sure I will! *(walks to side of stage and freezes.)*

(Partygoers sit on the floor and continue making subdued noise as narrator speaks.)

NARRATOR: King Belshazzar and his buddies partied all night and they got drunk. Then Belshazzar ordered a servant to bring in the gold and silver cups that his father, Nebuchadnezzar, had removed from God's temple in Jerusalem before the exile.
(Servant walks onstage with gold and silver cups and distributes them to the partygoers.)
He actually used these holy cups to toast their pagan idols! *(Party people raise cups.)*

*(Overhead projector shows on white wall and hand begins to write words. This can also be done by video projection of a hand writing on paper. All party people stop talking and stare at the wall. One drops his cup. All look terrified. These words
slowly appear on the wall: MENE, TEKEL, and PARSIN.)*

BELSHAZZAR: *(beginning to shake, looking as if he is about to fall)*
Wise men! Call for my wise men at once!
(Partygoers huddle together. Wise men run onstage and get close to stare at the wall.)

KING: Read this and interpret it for me. I will give you a purple robe, a gold chain, and a ruling position in my government if you can tell me what this means!

(Each wise man walks closer, looks at the words and then shaking his head, walks back and stops looking down at the ground as the narrator speaks).

NARRATOR: But as each wise man looked, he said nothing. Each just shook his head. No one could interpret the words. It's too bad that King Belshazzar, had not bothered to learn the key support people behind the throne. He did not know of Daniel's past success in helping the previous king.

WISE MAN SPEAKER: King Belshazzar, The queen once told me your father, Nebuchadnezzar, relied on an exile because his God blessed him. He could interpret dreams like no one else.

BELSHAZZAR: Send for this person, and hurry! *(Crumples to his knees.)*
(Partygoers put cups down and leave stage quickly and in fear.)

DANIEL: *(Comes to life at side of stage and walks to face audience where he speaks.)*
The King has summoned me! Let see what the poor man needs now. *(Walks slowly over to look at the words. Then he turns and faces the King who is still on his knees.)*

DANIEL continues: Oh, King Belshazzar. (Shakes head and continues speaking confidently)
God gave your father, Nebuchadnezzar, this great kingdom as well as honor. Now you, his son, have not showed the same spirit of a humble heart like your father grew to have. Look! *(Points to gold and silver cups)* Here you even drink from the holy cups that you stole from God's temple in Jerusalem! You know no shame! You have refused the God your father recognized as great. You have yet to humble yourself before that God. And now your time is up. Our great God has sent you *(Turns and points to wall)* these words.

KING: Please, tell me! What do they mean?

DANIEL: "Mene" means numbered. God has numbered the days of your kingdom and this is it. You've reached the last day. *(The King cries out.)* "Jekel" means weighed. You have been weighed on God's scale. You have come up lacking in what a king needs to have. *(Another wail from the king)* "Parsinmeans" means divided. God has divided your kingdom between the Medes and the Persians. *(King utters a soft moan, then stands and faces Daniel.)*

BELSHAZZAR: You have answered my question. *(Reaches behind his throne and gets purple robe and gold chain which he hands to Daniel.)* Daniel. You are now the third in command in my kingdom.
Shoulders slumped and head down, the King leaves the stage.
Daniel leaves stage and more makeup is added to make him look older. Stage lights go off. White wall on which words were written is removed. Distant battle sound effects are heard as narrator reads.

NARRATOR: King Belshazzar was killed that night. Cyrus led the Persians against the Babylonian Empire and Darius was made King.

(King Darius walks onstage and sits on the throne. Stage lights go on.)

NARRATOR continues: King Darius divided his new kingdom real estate into 120 states. One governor was assigned to govern each state. Three officials looked over the 120 governors. Daniel is one of the three top officials. Daniel is now in his 80's, yet still very good at everything he does.

(Daniel enters looking older and walking slower-walks across the stage to where King Darius sits. Two Persians enter and walk towards the King's throne)

KING DARIUS: *(taking to Daniel as 2 Persians walk by and overhear)* Daniel, you've done such an excellent job; I'm putting you in charge of the whole kingdom! *(King freezes as he reaches out his arm pointing in the direction of an imaginary window.)*

DANIEL: I will do my best, King Darius. *(Daniel enters, looking older and walking slower, and walks over to side stage and appears to look through the imaginary window, and then kneels in prayer.)*

PERSIAN #1: Did you hear that? *(Pointing towards the King who is frozen in place)* The King says that old Israelite exile, Daniel, is going to tell all of us what to do!

PERSIAN #2: I sure did. It's not fair!

PERSIAN #1: What can we do about it? We've already tried to find something that would get Daniel in trouble... something bad that he's done. But there's nothing! He's just too good to be real.

PERSIAN #2: Wait! There just might be if we look at that religion of his. We'll have to be clever and set up the King in this matter. *(Whispers in the ear of Persian #1 who nods in agreement.)*

(The two Persians strut over to the King who now looks up.)

PERSIAN #1: Oh great King Darius! We have news for you. All of your officials feel that you should be honored and praised. For the next 30 days it should be against the law for anyone in your kingdom to pray to any god or man, except you!

KING DARIUS: And what if they don't follow this law?

PERSIAN #2: Anyone who disobeys would be thrown into a den of lions.

KING DARIUS: Lions?

PERSIAN #1: Yes, King Darius, lions.

KING DARIUS: Well, if so many of my leaders think this is important, I declare it to be a law.

(King lowers his head and freezes while sitting on the throne. The Persians hide their smiles.)

NARRATOR: The Persian officials are thrilled because their plot against Daniel is in motion.

(They go over to each corner of the stage facing the audience and proclaim the new law simultaneously. Daniel rises from his prayer and walks over to hear what they are proclaiming.)

PERSIANS #1 and #2: The King has declared a new law. For the next thirty days no one is allowed to pray to anyone or anything, unless it is to King Darius himself. Anyone who disobeys will be thrown into a den filled with lions! *(Both growl, and put hands up like a lion would, then laugh cruelly as they leave the stage.)*

(As soon as they finish Daniel shakes his head 'no' and returns to face the imaginary window.)

NARRATOR: Daniel heard the new law. He knew that if he prayed to the God of the Israelites he would be thrown to the lions. After all these years, what do you think Daniel did? *(Audience response may be invited.)*

(Daniel kneels in prayer.)

NARRATOR continues: Yes, Daniel stayed true to his God, the one true God. Daniel's God had walked with him during all his days in Babylonian exile. This was the same God who walked through the fire with Shadrach, Meshach, and Abednego, and who interpreted dreams of two kings. Daniel truly put God first in his life. Daniel prayed that day and he continued three times a day, until one day....

(PERSIANS #1 and #2 walk onstage and sneak up behind Daniel who still kneels in prayer.)

PERSIAN #1: Aha! Gotcha!

PERSIAN #2: Wait until King Darius hears that his top official is breaking the law! Daniel's praying to someone other than the King!

PERSIAN #1: *(Roughly pulls Daniel to his feet.)* You're coming with us to report to this to the King!

(The three walk over to where King Darius is seated. King moves to life again.)

PERSIAN #2: King Darius, didn't you proclaim a law that forbade prayer to anyone but you yourself, and no one else, for 30 days?

KING DARIUS: *(Looking at Daniel and speaking slowly to him first)* Hello, Daniel, my friend. *(Slowly looking back at the Persians)* Yes, I did, at your recommendation!

PERSIAN #1: And the punishment for not obeying was to be thrown into a den with lions, right?

KING DARIUS: *(leans back in his chair as if wanting to back away and gives a drawn out answer)* Yeesss. *(Pause)* Why do you ask?

PERSIAN #2: Well, Your Highness, this *(points at Daniel)* Israelite captive, who you made a top official in your kingdom, has broken your law!

PERSIAN #1: He continues to pray to his God. And he does it three times a day!

KING DARIUS: *(puts his hands over his eyes realizing the situation)* Oh no, Daniel! What can be done to make an exception for Daniel?

PERSIAN #2: *(Simultaneously and loudly)* Nothing!

PERSIAN #1: *(Haughtily)* And remember, King Darius, not even you can change the law! It is your law!

KING DARIUS: So Daniel, my most trusted and most capable official, must go to the lions . . .

(The king stands and slowly walks over to Daniel. He puts his hands on Daniel's shoulders as he speaks. The King looks very upset.)

KING DARIUS: Daniel, you have been as faithful to me in your work as you have been to your obedience to your God. I pray that your God will rescue you from these lions!

(The King backs offstage as stage lights go off.
Throne is removed and lion's den is brought in with 2 step ladders.
One ladder is put inside den. If preferred, a front den opening may be used.
Stage lights go on as two Persians take Daniel by the arms and lead him to the lion's den. Daniel climbs a ladder to get in. The guards help Daniel up the ladder.
Recorded sounds of lions are heard. There is no talking as Daniel enters the lion's den.)

(Two Persians then cover the den opening with a cover that may be a sheet
The King returns to the opposite side of the stage, holding his head in great sadness. Persians stand guard by the den. Stage lights dim to represent night.
Roaring dies out as narration begins.)

NARRATOR: King Darius was so upset by this turn of events that he could not sleep that night.
(King paces back and forth. A rooster is heard offstage, and stage lights go on.)
At daybreak the King raced to the lion's den.

(King runs to the den where now there are no sounds. He calls out to Daniel.)

KING DARIUS: *(loudly)* Daniel! Has your God saved you from the lions?

DANIEL: Yes, King Darius! My God sent an angel to shut the mouths of the lions so they could not hurt me. My God knew I was blameless. Just like you know it, King Darius!

KING DARIUS: *(looking at the two Persians)* You two! Help Daniel out!
(The Persians pull Daniel out and help him down to where the King hugs him at the bottom of the ladder. Then the King turns on the Persians.)

KING DARIUS: And as for you... You who set Daniel up for this. Now you will both go into the lion's den. *(Extra guards push the two into the den.)*

NARRATOR: This time, no one shut the mouths of the lions. The men, who tricked the King and set up one of God's faithful children, were sent to death.

KING DARIUS: *(speaking to audience)* From now on, everyone in my kingdom, including you, must fear and honor the God of Daniel, the God of the Israelites. This God alone is the living God, the one true God. His Kingdom will last forever. The God who saved Daniel from the lions will be in power over all, forever!

(Stage lights of off as narration continues. Lion's den and ladders are removed.)

NARRATOR: Hope was given in the wonderful works of God in Daniel's time. All of God's children who listened were reminded that their God was with them. Their God loved them and protected them. Daniel remembered this as he lived on into the reign of King Cyrus. It was during this time that Daniel's dream came true... the Israelites were finally allowed to return to their cherished Promised Land of Judah in 583 B.C....which is when our story began with Daniel. Do the people understand God's love and promise to stay with them?
Do they believe that God walks with us in the fires of life? Do they believe that He protects us all against the lions that threaten to destroy us? Yes, God loves them still, just as He still loves us today. What a great and mighty God we have!

THE END

SHADRACH, MESHACH, AND ABEDNEGO
Daniel 1-3

CAST (Grouped by measure of involvement in play, most to least)
***Actors can double up on these parts.*

SPEAKING PARTS

Narrator: Adult
King Nebuchadnezzar: Adult or older boy
Shadrach: Older teen boy ("S" appears on front of his outfit)
Meshach: Older teen boy ("M" appears on front of his outfit)
Abednego: Older teen boy ("A" appears on front of his outfit)
Daniel: Older teen boy ("D" appears on front of his outfit)
Man #1: Any age**
Man #2: Any age**
King's servant: Any age**
Food server guard: Any age**
Guard #1: Any age (who blows horn)**
Guard #2: Any age**

NONSPEAKING PARTS

4-5 young men: About age of Shadrach, Meshach, Abednego, Daniel
Server #2: Any age**
Statue carrier: Any age**
2 strong guards: Any age**
5+ Exiles in ragged clothing: Mixed ages
Extras: Any age** (who observe statue)
Extras: Any age** (who move flames)

STAGE

All scenes are done on a central stage area.

SETTING

The opening scene is a mural of a desert. A table, with 4 scrolls placed below the table, is set at the right side of the stage. A furnace of cardboard is constructed and stapled together so that if is 3 dimensional and will accommodate 3-5 people. A window opening is painted on the furnace where the King can observe the three. Two stepladders, one inside the furnace, and one outside, to be used to climb in and out of the furnace are placed.

PROPS

- 4 bowls of dry ice and water (add water just before putting on stage).
- 5 scrolls
- Glasses
- Horn
- King's throne
- Large gold statue
- Pitchers
- Poster board flames
- Roaring fire sound effects
- Stage light with red filter
- Tape measure
- Trays
- Vegetables

SHADRACH, MESHACH, AND ABEDNEGO
The Play Begins

NARRATOR: During their years of exile, God spoke to the Children of Israel. Again and again, the prophets reminded them to follow the Ten Commandments; to choose good over evil; to sacrifice correctly; and to follow Him, the one and only true God. Elijah, Elisha, Isaiah, Jonah, Ezekiel, and Jeremiah spread the message. But did anyone listen? Did they hear God through the prophets? Did the Children of Israel remember their past experiences of being taken over and ruled by foreigners? Did they remember Moses? Did they remember all that bad that happened when they turned away from their one true God over the years?

(A line of at least five ragged exiles plod across the stage. They stop to catch their breath. Once seated one of the exiles begins to sob softly, two others join in except for the two men who begin to talk. Muffled crying is heard throughout their dialogue.)

NARRATOR continues: It looks like the Children of Israel have messed up again.

MAN #1: I knew we should have listened to that prophet, Jeremiah!

MAN #2: Hindsight is always the best. We're both a bit late to realize that!

MAN #1: Jeremiah said the Babylonians would return and finish off Jerusalem.

MAN #2: He also said it would be better to give up and spend our 70 years of punishment in Babylon. I hope he was right!

MAN #1: The last I heard of Jeremiah he was being punished by being stuck deep in a dark pit filled with mud and filth. Who knows what's right?

MAN #2: All I know is that I'm scared to death! Did you see what the Babylonians did to our city? Do you believe they tore down the temple King Solomon built?

MAN #1: At least they took the gold and silver holy objects out of the temple before they destroyed it. You can be sure it will end up in one of their pagan temples! It makes my blood run cold just thinking of it! *(Shivers)*

MAN #2: *(Startled - point as he speaks)* Turn around! Do you see that thin line of smoke?

MAN #1: Is the city burning? Is David's city burning? Oh! Jerusalem!

MAN #2: I knew it! Once the Babylonians emptied most of the city and marched us into exile, they planned to burn it to the ground. Only rubble will be left if they have their way.

MAN #1: And ashes. .

MAN #2: We at least have memories of what we had... *(Man #1 interrupts.)*

MAN #1: And knowledge of what we lost because we didn't follow God's directions!

(Both now cover their faces and rock back and forth in mourning, joining the others. After a short time all rise and walk off the stage as the narrator continues.)

NARRATOR: The exiles walked almost one thousand miles from Jerusalem to Babylon, leaving behind the land God promised Abraham, Isaac, and Jacob. Canaan, the Promised Land, was now desolate.

(Stage lights go off and desert mural is removed and furnace is put on stage. Stage lights go on. A line of young men, including Shadrach, Meshach, Abednego and Daniel enter and line up facing the audience. They are easily spotted because of the initials on their outfits. A guard comes on stage and moves the young men around in the line while the narrator continues speaking. Shadrach, Meshach, Abednego, and Daniel stay together in the center.)

NARRATOR continues: Many of the Children of Israel ended up doing work similar to what they had done in Jerusalem. Some ended up doing hard physical labor. Some were craftsmen. Some were shopkeepers. And some were specially chosen to be officers in the king's palace.

(King's Servant walks up and down with open scroll - a clipboard may be used - as he makes notes on it while standing in front of each man. He stands back and speaks.)

KING'S SERVANT: You have been tested to see which of you are the most fit to work in the king's palace. According to the final tally, four of you have been chosen. Step forward when I call your name. *(Slowly and loudly)*
Shadrach! *(Shadrach steps forward, looking back at his three friends)*
Meshach! *(Meshach steps next to Shadrach and they look at each other. then back at the other two.)*
Abednego! *(Abednego joins the two and they give each other a quick shoulder pat. Then they look back at Daniel.)*
And the young man with the highest grades, so far- Daniel! *(Daniel sprints up, and they give each other the "high 5.")*

KING'S SERVANT continues: You four will immediately begin learning the Babylonian language as well as all our customs and ways of life. You will be educated in King Nebuchadnezzar's Academy for three years. Then you will work as officials of King Nebuchadnezzar in Babylon. *(The four clasp hands joyfully. Servant points at Daniel, Shadrach, Meshach, and Abednego.)* Please be seated at the table and await further directions.
(The guard turns to the others as the four sit at the table.) The rest of you, follow me.

(As the narrator begins to speak all follow the servant except the four who sit at a table at the right side of the stage area.)

NARRATOR: Life looked good for the four friends until mealtime. The Children of Israel were served the same food that was prepared for the King's table. *(Food server guard enters with a tray of food and sets it on the table. The four stare at it then three of them look at Daniel.)* What they saw was food prepared in pagan ways, not the way the God of Israel told His children to prepare their food. They all saw the problem and looked at Daniel. Daniel immediately took charge and spoke for them.

DANIEL: May I stand and speak, Sir?

FOOD SERVER GUARD: You may.

DANIEL: I must tell you that this food is on our "Forbidden Foods list" that we were taught not to eat when we lived in Judah. Please allow us to eat food that does not go against our beliefs.

NARRATOR: God softened the server's heart.

FOOD SERVER GUARD: Hmm. I believe your words, but I am afraid to do so. At the end of this test, the King will have my head on a platter if you are not as strong as the other group that will be eating his food! *(Pointing to his own head, then the food platter.)*

DANIEL: Sir, don't you like a healthy competition? Would you test us for, let's say, ten days? Just serve us vegetables and water.

FOOD SERVER GUARD: Just vegetables and water?

DANIEL: Yes. Then, at the end of the ten-day contest compare us to the others who ate the King's food.

FOOD SERVER GUARD: Well, you are in good shape to start with... All right. Just for ten days, veggies and water it will be!

(Server snaps fingers and Server #2 brings a tray of vegetables in along with pitchers of water. The four appear to gobble the food while the servers leave the stage.)

NARRATOR: The guard keeps to his word for the next ten days. Then it was time for the test.

(Food Server Guard returns to the table where the 4 are seated. They put food and glasses down, lean back and pat their stomachs. He mumbles as the food server guard takes out a tape measure and measures the biceps of each. He then turns to address the audience.)

FOOD SERVER GUARD: Not only have these four proved to be stronger, but other tests show they're also smarter! I see a great future for these four!

(The four friends pantomime congratulating each other. Food Server Guard and servant walk back and shake their hands before departing. Daniel then passes out scrolls - which are under the table. As the narrator speaks they quietly open the scrolls and read.)

NARRATOR: And so it happened. Daniel, especially, stood out above the others. Years from now King Nebuchadnezzar will appoint Daniel to rule over all Babylon. Daniel will remember his friends, and at his request they will be promoted to work with him. Life will move along smoothly. The four will stay true to the God of the Israelites, just as they stay loyal to each other. But now, back to where we left off . . .

(The four stand as statue carrier and guards #1 and #2 walk on stage with a large gold statue. Guard #1 has a horn. Daniel leaves the stage. The other three turn and watch as the statue is placed on the ground. King Nebuchadnezzar and extras follow the statue in and admire it. Guard #1 loudly blows a horn to get the people's attention. He then steps to face the audience and proclaims the King's message. The three quietly watch from the table.)

GUARD #1: This is the King's command. All people: When the horn is blown during the day you must fall down and worship this (points to statue) golden image that King Nebuchadnezzar has set up. Anyone who does not bow down will be thrown into a blazing furnace!

(Guard # 1 blows horn again. All fall down, except the two guards, the king who is admiring the statue, and Daniel's three friends. The three friends stand, turn, and begin to walk offstage; as they pass by the statue they glance briefly at it before leaving the stage. The guards follow them with their eyes. Both rush over to the King who is still admiring the statue.)

GUARD #1 with horn: *(speaking quickly)* King Nebuchadnezzar! You should know that there are three Israelite exiles working for you in big palace jobs who aren't paying attention to your new orders.

KING: What are you saying?

GUARD #1: They are not serving your god, Your Majesty!

GUARD #2: And now they do not worship the statue of gold you just put up!

KING: What? *(He clenches his fists).* Bring them to me, now! *(King paces back and forth.)*

(The two guards run offstage and bring the three back onto the stage holding them by the arms. They all walk back to the King who now has his hands on his hips in anger.)

GUARD #2: These are the three Israelites who refuse to worship the gold statue, Your Majesty.

KING: Shadrach! Meshach! Abednego! These guards tell me you did not fall down in front of the gold statue as I commanded. I will ignore it this time, but if you do not worship the statue you must be punished like everyone else. You must go into the fiery furnace! Tell me, what god will take the heat off of you then? What god will rescue you? Ha!

(Furnace sounds are turned on low for background noise.)

SHADRACH: Oh, King! We don't have to defend ourselves.

MESHACH: If we're thrown into the blazing furnace, our God will save us from the fire, as well as from you!

ABEDNEGO: And even if our God does not save us, we still will not serve your gods or worship the image of gold you set up.

(The King goes into a rage, stomping his feet and screaming.)

KING: Heat the fire seven times hotter! Then throw these three into the fire!

(Stage lights begin to dim as the King stomps offstage. Guards easily lead the three offstage. The table and chairs are removed and the furnace - people (holding posters of flames) get inside the furnace to make the flames dance.)

(Ladders are put on each side of the furnace wall, and 4 bowls of water and dry ice are put inside the furnace to create smoke. Stage lights come on as the guards bring the three back on stage.)

(The three climb up the ladder next to the furnace wall and go down into the furnace using another ladder placed inside. Flame holders hold up poster to shoot up from behind the furnace wall.)

(The sound of roaring Flames is turned on high over a sound system. Red filter over stage lights gives a heated effect. The King enters from the other side of the stage and watches. Then he rushes to viewing-window on the side of the furnace, puts his eye up to it, throws hands in air, freezes momentarily, and runs over to address the audience. The roaring flame sound softens so he can be heard.)

KING: Didn't we just put three men in the fire? *(Audience may be prompted to respond.)* But now there are FOUR! How can there be four? And one of them looks like a god! *(The King runs to the fire pit and climbs to the top of the ladder himself. Looking over into the furnace he calls out)* Shadrach! Meshach! Abednego! You servants of the Most High God! Come out! Come out, now!
(All available actors rush up on stage. As the three come out of the furnace each is grabbed and checked for bums and sniffed for the scent of smoke. All, except the three friends are seen shrugging and shaking their heads in confusion.)

GUARD #1: They don't even smell like smoke!

KING: Praise the God of Shadrach, Meshach, and Abednego! These three Israelites trusted in their God enough to defy my command! They were ready to give up their own lives rather than disobey their God.

(All actors on stage mumble as they point nervously at the three.)

KING continues: Therefore, I declare this: No one shall speak against the God of Shadrach, Meshach, and Abednego, because no other god can save like their God can! We have seen it!

NARRATOR: Not only did God give Shadrach, Meshach, and Abednego strength to stand up for their beliefs, He walked with them through the fire of punishment. That they willingly walked through the fire was proof to other exiles from the Promised Land, as well as pagans, that the God of the Israelites was real and still at their side. What a lesson for the pagan King Nebuchadnezzar! And what a miracle it was to see God's presence alive and well through the courage and faith of these extraordinary young men of God. They remembered, and we should all remember this truth: No matter what fire we walk through, God walks with us.
We are never, ever alone.

THE END

ESTHER
Esther 1-10

CAST (Grouped by measure of involvement in play, most to least.)
***Actors can double up on these parts.*

SPEAKING PARTS

Narrator: Adult - will read connecting explanations between dialogues
King Xerxes: Older boy
Queen Esther: Older girl
Mordecai: Older boy
Haman: Older boy. This person should show cunning and meanness
Messenger: Any age**
Queen Vashti: Older girl
Advisor #1: Any age**
Advisor #2: Any age**
King's servant: Any age**
Queen Esther's servant: Girl, any age**
Officer #1: Any age**
Officer #2: Any age**
Haman's wife: Any age**
Guard #1: Any age**
Guard #2: Any age**

NONSPEAKING PARTS

Messengers: (who ride broom horses) Any age**
Women at Queen Vashti's table: (3) Any age**
Men at the King's table: (3) Any age - the "party-goers")
Potential queens: (4) Any age
Men dressed in dark clothes: (2) Any age

STAGE

All early scenes take place on stage as it switches between palace and garden.

SETTING

Three backgrounds are represented.
1. Palace background shows blue and white curtains with purple cord ties in silver rings fastened to marble columns. A piece of two-sided tape attached for future use on one column. Silver and gold couches could be painted.
2. A garden background shows a trellis, flowering bushes, and trees.
3. A background reflection or overhead projection would show a tower with a rope hanging down.

- 1 Horse headdress
- 2 Card tables with 4 chairs around each
- 2 Crowns, one for King Xerxes and one for Queen Esther
- 2 Stick horses
- 2 Table coverings
- 3 Royal capes in different colors
- 3 Scroll messages to hand out
- 5 Hand mirrors
- 8 Gold cups
- 8 Large table pieces
- Finger ring - large / gaudy enough to be visible to the audience
- Large food props such as fruit, vegetables, meat
- Large metal cups or goblets
- Large hand drawn or professional wall map or projection of the Persian Empire including Egypt to India
- Large note pad
- Large pillow
- Large quill pens
- Large scrolls 2
- Party noise soundtrack
- Royal capes for officials
- Sign that says "3 DAYS LATER"
- Small baggy of gold glitter
- Unbreakable cup that can be thrown on floor
- Wood pieces for casting lots

STAGE SETTING

Stage is dark as Narrator begins to talk. Stage lights come on to show map of Persian Kingdom.

NOTE: If lighting cannot be controlled, then stage-hands can quickly move backgrounds and props on and off the stage.

ESTHER - The Play Begins

NARRATOR: King Xerxes I ruled between 485 BC and 465 BC. He was young king who ruled over the huge Persian Kingdom that stretched from Egypt to India. *(Points to map)* Persia *(sweep map)* was made up of 127 provinces. King Xerxes ruled over all of them. The area was so big that a mail system had been set up earlier by King Darius to get messages across the kingdom quickly using messengers on horses . . . like these two messenger teams, who were known for their speed. *(Two messengers run in on stick horses from opposite sides and pass each other, then turn around and run across the stage a second time.)*

NARRATOR continues: Using special horses, the messengers were able to cover 1,677 miles - in seven days! It was a Persian Pony Express! These riders delivered all kinds of messages, even dinner invitations!

(Stage lights go off and palace background is put in place. One table, 4 chairs, food and props are moved into place on right side. A second table and 4 chairs are placed on left side with Garden Backdrop being added. NOTE: Both backdrops are up at the same time. Stage lights go on.)

KING XERXES: *(King enters with other partygoers holding beverage goblets; all 4 sit at table set for dinner. The King holds up a goblet in a toast.)* I hope you, my officials, my officers, governors, and army commanders enjoy your stay here. My kingdom is so great I don't know where to begin! *(King and guests begin to quietly talk.)*

NARRATOR: The king did find a place to begin, and he didn't stop entertaining for 180 days! *(First group of 3 men leave table and walk over to sit at the table in front of garden backdrop. Queen Vashti walks on stage with 3 women to replace them at the first table.)*

NARRATOR continues: This time he invited everyone in the capital city of Susa. *(Background party sounds are heard).* For seven days they ate and drank in the palace garden while Queen Vashti entertained inside the palace. By the seventh day of partying the happy King had an idea. *(King stands and throws his arms up).* Messenger!
(Speaking messenger runs over and listens as the King whispers in his ear; he runs over to the Queen.)

MESSENGER: *(to Queen Vashti)* Queen Vashti, the King of Persia, King Xerxes, wants you to come over to his party. He wants you to wear your crown and show off your beauty to his guests.

QUEEN VASHTI: *(stands in a huff and shouts)* No! I've had it with the king, his bragging, and his telling me what to do! Tell him I will NOT go to him!

(Messenger looks shocked, turns and runs back to the King. Women at the queen's table stand and pat her on the back in agreement with what she has done.)

MESSENGER: *(speaks to the King who is laughing)* The Queen, she says . . . "No!"

(King's face drops and the others around him stop cold and listen. Messenger backs off and stands quietly.)

KING XERXES: Call my advisors over here! I can't think straight! I need legal advice, and now! *(Two advisors walk up to the King.)*

KING XERXES continues: *(to advisors)* My queen, Queen Vashti, refused to come to me when I sent for her. What are my legal rights? What do you advise?

ADVISOR #1: Well, first of all, she has embarrassed you as well as insulted your guests.

ADVISOR #2: When news of her refusal spreads, other wives will think they don't have to obey their husbands! That's unthinkable!

ADVISOR #1: Then those wives will not respect their husbands, and the husbands will get angry.

ADVISOR #2: My advice, Your Highness, is for you to write a permanent law that will keep Queen Vashti from ever seeing you again. Then you can replace her with someone who respects and obeys you.

ADVISOR #1: Wives across your kingdom will see this. Then they will respect and obey their husbands.

KING XERXES: Yes! That does sound good! Husbands should have complete control over wives and families. Yes, I like that! *(He writes rapidly on a scroll, which he takes from the table)* Messenger! Come here now! *(Messenger goes to King)* Get this news out immediately. Queen Vashti is history! Husbands rule their homes in Persia!

(Messenger takes scroll and runs offstage. All other actors follow the messenger leaving the King, who sits at his table and hold his head in his hands as if upset. Servant enters and walks up to the King who still looks downcast. Stage hands may remove Queen's table, chairs and garden backdrop.)

SERVANT: Your Highness, it is time to find another queen for your kingdom. Why not have beautiful women from every province come to the palace? Once they arrive here they can visit the beauty "spa" before they meet you. You can choose your next queen from the most beautiful women in your kingdom!

(King Xerxes slowly raises his head to look at the servant as he (Xerxes) speaks. Then the King jumps up.)

KING XERXES: I like that idea! *(Claps his hands joyfully)* Let's begin the search immediately!

(Both run offstage)

(Mordecai and Esther walk toward stage from the audience. They stop just before entering the stage. Mordecai hugs Esther as in farewell.)

MORDECAI: Esther, my dear, we are cousins; but you know that when your parents died, I raised you as a daughter. You must answer the King's call for beautiful women. It is good-bye just for now. But remember, you and your relatives are Children of Israel. Nebuchadnezzar took us captive from Jerusalem, and we have lived here in Babylon ever since. Know this in your heart, but keep it a secret. Tell no one that you are an Israelite!

(4 potential queens walk in from where Esther and Mordecai have entered. They pass by Esther and Mordecai and walk up to the palace background. They are giggling, looking in hand mirrors, and admiring themselves. Esther slowly leaves Mordecai and walks to where the girls are lined up. She shyly looks at the ground as the other girls talk.)

(The King and his servant walk in from right side of the stage. This servant is carrying a notepad, crown, and baggy of gold glitter. The King begins to look carefully at each girl and he whispers to his note-taking servant, before going on to the next girl. Mordecai walks down to the audience level and paces back and forth nervously in front of the audience, unaware of what is happening. When the King walks up to Esther his servant inconspicuously tosses gold sparkles in the air. The king shakes and stops as he stares at Esther before speaking.)

KING XERXES: I have found you! Finally, I have found my new queen!

(Takes crown from servant and puts it on her head.)

(Extras enter stage cheering as they crowd around Esther. Rejected girls look down as they exit the stage. Mordecai is still pacing in front of the audience. The servant walks to the edge of the stage to face the audience, cups his hand and proclaims the news.)

SERVANT: The queen has been chosen! *(Mordecai stops and turns to hear the news.)* Our new queen is named Queen Esther!

MORDECAI: *(starts jumping up and down screaming)* Esther! Esther! Queen Esther! *(He then invites the audience to join in his joy.)* Esther! Queen Esther!

SERVANT: *(continuing)* And in honor of the new Queen, the King announces a dinner party and a holiday throughout the kingdom!

MORDECAI: *(Inviting audience to join him)* Long live Queen Esther! Long live Queen Esther!

(All leave stage. Mordecai runs back stage, puts on a royal cap, and returns to the stage. Two men dressed in dark clothes sneakily enter the stage near the palace backdrop where they stop and whisper secretly as the narrator begins to read. We see Mordecai watching them from a distance.)

NARRATOR: In time Mordecai found a job working inside the palace. One day he overhears a plot to kill the King!

MORDECAI: *(to audience)* I must tell Esther! *(He turns to run offstage left and he bumps into Esther who has come on stage. He points to the men in dark clothes and whispers in Esther's ear. All run off stage as the narrator speaks.)*

NARRATOR: Sure enough, the king was told, the plot was investigated, and it was for real! Because of their plans to kill the king, those men were killed. *(King enters and walks around the stage with servant who is writing as they walk.)* The king liked to keep a record of the events that took place in his kingdom so he made sure this was added. *(Servant finishes writing and leaves stage right. Haman enters and walks over to the King.)*

HAMAN: *(waving to the king)* King Xerxes, your Highness! Greetings!

KING XERXES: *(waving back)* Hello, Haman, my trusted advisor and friend! So much is happening. My kingdom is so busy with so many things going on; dinners, divorce, beauty contests, new queen, more dinners, holidays, murder plots. Oh there's so much to keep track of! I'm glad you're here because I have wanted to promote you to the highest office in my kingdom -- next to me, of course!

HAMAN: *(hugging himself and bowing)* Oh your Highness, thank you, King Xerxes!

KING XERXES: And from now on all other officials must kneel down to honor you at the royal gate! Let us drink to your new position in Persia! *(King hands Haman a large plastic cup)*

HAMAN: *(Puts his arms in the air as he spins around and speaks)*
 Oh, this is too good to be true! Yes! Yes! Yes!
(King walks offstage and Haman stands with an overconfident look on his face, as officers 1 and 2 walk up to him, kneel, and continue walking away. Haman arrogantly raises his head. The last is Mordecai. He ignores Haman, but Haman doesn't see because he has his nose in the air.)

NARRATOR: Well, everyone got down on their knees for Haman. Everyone except Mordecai!
(Haman stands with his nose so high he does not see Mordecai walk by him. Officers rush up and shake Mordecai as they question him.)

OFFICER #1: Mordecai, you must kneel before Haman!

MORDECAI: I will not!

OFFICER #2: The king orders us all to kneel!

MORDECAI: I will not kneel before Haman!

OFFICER #1: Why?

MORDECAI: Because I am an Israelite! I will not bow down to Haman!
(Mordecai leaves stage.)

OFFICER#1: *(to other officer)* He's hopeless! Let's go tell Haman ourselves. Let's see what the great Haman will do! *(Officers walk over and kneel in front of Haman who slowly looks down and motions for them to rise after they cough to get his attention.)*

OFFICER #1: Haman, we honor you by bowing as the king has ordered, but one official does not.

OFFICER #2: And we knew you'd want to know...

HAMAN: *(interrupting)* Who is it? Who refuses to bow down to me? Who will not honor the King's directive?

OFFICERS: *(simultaneously)* It's Mordecai! Mordecai refuses to bow down to you!

(Haman throws unbreakable cup he's been holding on the ground, making a loud noise.)

HAMAN: *(enraged)* Mordecai, huh? My old "buddy" Mordecai?

OFFICER #1: We tried talking to him, but it was no use.

HAMAN: *(ponders and speaks)* We'll see about that! I'll fix him. *(ponders and speaks)*
No. Just getting rid of him won't be enough. I have to get rid of all of his relatives.
(Pauses again and speaks) I must get rid of all the Israelites in the kingdom!
(Turning to officers) I need your help to decide what day to make my move. Cast lots for me!

*(Both officers look in their pockets; Officer#1 finds pieces of wood and tosses them like dice.
He shows them to Haman.)*

HAMAN: Thank you, Officers!

(Officers leave stage and Haman walks toward the king who is returning from the other side.)

HAMAN continues: Greetings, king! May your most important official have a word with you?

KING XERXES: Of course. What is it Haman?

HAMAN; I have learned that there are some people who live in all areas of your kingdom who
are trouble-makers. They have different customs than ours. Worst of all, they refuse to obey
your orders! *(King looks concerned.)* Now, Your Highness, as your top official it is my duty to
make my recommendation to you. I think these people should be killed! Plus, I guarantee you'll
add tons of silver to your treasury when you take their money.

NARRATOR: Of course, Haman was making up a story that was not true, but the king didn't
know it. And since Haman made it sound so real, the king didn't give it much thought. He
didn't even ask who "these people" were! The king just gave the responsibility to Haman to
resolve the problem in his own way.

KING XERXES: Haman, do as you want. Take my royal stamping ring and place my stamp on
your decision to make it official. *(Takes ring from his hand and hands it to Haman.)* As for their
money, you keep it!

NARRATOR: Haman was thrilled. He immediately wrote the letters and sent them across the
kingdom. *(Haman pulls 3 messages from his outfit. He gives one to each of the messengers and
keeps one to read to himself.)*

HAMAN: *(reads aloud to audience)* "On the date written on this letter, all Israelite men,
women, and children are to be killed! Their property is to be taken!" *(Haman jumps in the air
with joy and runs over to the pillar where he sticks the letter on a two sided piece of tape.
Haman laughs and yells joyfully until he is offstage. He leaves stage as Mordecai comes on
stage. Mordecai walks by the letter, stops, reads, and falls to his knees. He turns to the
audience. Haman may still be heard hollering in the distance.)*

MORDECAI: *(sobbing) Oh*, my people! My people! My God! What are we to do? *(Sobs silently)* Esther! *(He stands suddenly)* I must get this to Esther. She must know about this letter! *(Looks around and sees a girl servant come on stage. He rushes to her and kneels.)*

MORDECAI continues: Please, please take this to Queen Esther! Tell her that her uncle sends it. And hurry! Tell her to beg the king for our lives and stand up for her people.

(Mordecai freezes on stage and Esther enters from the other side. The girl servant goes directly to her and hands her the letter.)

ESTHER: What is this? Ah, a letter. *(Begins to open it.)*

SERVANT GIRL: *(breaking in)* It is from your uncle, Queen Esther. He wants you to beg the king for our lives. He wants you to stand up for your people!

ESTHER: Oh, Mordecai! It must be important. Let's see... *(Begins to read silently)* Oh! Oh no! What is this? How can this be? *(Looks away)* Haman! I know Haman is behind this! And you said my uncle wants me to beg the King for our lives? Doesn't he know that even I can't go before the King without being invited, or I will be killed? I can't do it! Go back and tell him it's impossible! *(Esther freezes in place.)*

SERVANT: *(rushes over to Mordecai who becomes alert on the other side of the stage)* Queen Esther says that she can't talk to the king unless she's invited. Or else she could be killed! She says it's impossible!

MORDECAI: *(Clenching hands, acting frustrated)* She will not be safe just because she's inside the palace! But, tell her she must speak up or she and her whole family will be killed. Also tell her- *(He whispers in servant's ear.)* Can you remember all that?
(Girl nods and runs to Esther. Mordecai freezes.)

SERVANT GIRL: Queen Esther, Mordecai said you must speak now or you and your family will be killed.

ESTHER: *(wringing hands in anguish)* But, but....

SERVANT GIRL: Mordecai also said, and he told me to say this exactly, "It could be that you were made Queen for a time as this!"

ESTHER: Oh... I never thought..."like this"... *(She hides her face in her hands for a few seconds, then drops her hands and speaks boldly.)* All right! I'll go to the king. Tell Mordecai to have all the Children of Israel in this city fast for 3 days to support me.

(Stage lights go off. All leave stage off one side while sign carrier walks across stage with sign, "3 DAYS LATER". Stagehands moves two tables and chairs in place at opposite sides of the stage. Stage lights go on as king enters from one side, goes to his table and sits. Queen enters from other side. She stops, stares ahead, takes a deep breath and approaches the king who looks up.)

KING: Esther! What a surprise! I didn't invite you, and you know what that means! But *(he shrugs)* come on in anyway. I haven't seen you for days! What can I do for you?

ESTHER: *(breathing a visible sigh of relief)* Oh, Your Highness, I would like to make a special dinner for you. And why don't you bring Haman along, too?

KING XERXES: Dinner! Party time! Yes, of course. We'll be there!
(Stage lights go off as King leaves stage and Esther goes to sit at her table.)

NARRATOR: Of course, the king was there with his second in command, Haman.
(Lights go up as King and Haman join Esther who is sitting at her table.)
He loves parties and was so happy that he asked what Esther wanted.

KING XERXES: Esther. This dinner is wonderful. What would you like? I'll give you up to half of my kingdom!

ESTHER: Hmmm. What I'd really like is for you and Haman to come to dinner again tomorrow night! Then, I'll tell you what you can do for me.

NARRATOR: Does Esther think that the way to a king's heart is through his stomach? She definitely has a plan! In the meantime, Haman struts home where he brags about his importance and his irritation.

HAMAN: *(Haman leaves Esther and the king at the table; struts out to face audience to speak)* I am so rich, between my money and my sons... And the king, he thinks I'm just wonderful! The others all look up to me and bow to me. Why, even Queen Esther! She thinks enough of me to invite me to a dinner with the king! She has her priorities straight! But there is one person that really bugs me. Mordecai! That Israelite who works in the palace is the only one who refuses to bow down to me like the King ordered. As long as he's in the picture, I'm NOT HAPPY *(Stomps foot and yells)* I must deal with him, and soon!

(Haman's wife walks up from the audience)

HAMAN'S WIFE: Husband, I couldn't help but hear your complaint. Why not build a tower, say 75' tall tower. Tomorrow morning ask the king to hang Mordecai there. It will be all set up and ready to go. Then you'll be able to enjoy your dinner with the king and queen tomorrow night.
(Haman slowly nods. They leave the stage and the stage lights go off.)

(While the narrator reads, a reflection of the hanging gallows is shown on the background. The King comes out and lies down on the floor - head on pillow - unaware of Haman's plan against Mordecai. The stage lights go on dimly. A servant follows with a scroll and begins reading to him. Before the servant reads, the reflection of the gallows is turned off.)

NARRATOR: And so the tower was built. But meanwhile, back in the palace, the king could not sleep. Could it have been from overeating? Whatever the cause, when he can't sleep he has a servant read the events from his journal of "king related happenings". The servant has just read of the time when Mordecai found out about and stopped the two men who were plotting to kill the king.

(The king sits up straight.)

KING XERXES: Oh, yes! I remember that! Mordecai learned of a plot to kill me. He passed this information on and he was right! He saved my life. Servant, look again and tell me how I rewarded Mordecai.

SERVANT: *(Servants scan scroll with his finger.)* Your Highness, it does not say. I don't believe Mordecai received any thanks from you.

KING XERXES: Then I must do it! Let me think . . . how should I reward such a great man as Mordecai?

(A rooster crows offstage signifying dawn. The servant yawns. Stage lights are turned on bright. Haman struts on stage and over to the king.)

HAMAN: Good morning, king! I must ask you-- *(King interrupts him.)*

KING XERXES: Before you speak I need advice from you, my top official!
(Haman throws his head and shoulders back and sticks his chest out. Looking at the audience he points to himself.) What should I do to honor a special person? What do you think, Haman?

NARRATOR: Of course, Haman thought the king was speaking of Haman, himself!

HAMAN: Oh, king! That's easy! *(Struts around as he continues to speak)* Have the special person ride through the city on one of your best horses. The horse should wear one of its fancy headdresses. One of your highest officials will place the robe on the special person. That high official will lead the horse carrying the honored man, through the city while shouting, "This is how our king honors a man!"

(Haman stops strutting, throws his head and arms out and shouts.) Yes!

KING XERXES: Excellent thinking, Haman. That's why you're my top man! Get ready, and do this now. Do it for Mordecai! *(Servant leaves and King freezes.)*

HAMAN: Ehhhhhhhh!!! *(Arms, face, and body go limp as he stares at the King.)* Wh...What! M...M...M...Mor...Mor...de...cai!

(Stage lights go off. The king and Haman leave stage. Mordecai puts on a royal robe and climbs on a "stick horse" which is decorated with a royal looking headdress. Stage lights go on as Mordecai and Haman come back on stage. Haman leads Mordecai and his horse across the stage twice while continuously calling out the king's words. Mordecai waves at the audience.)

HAMAN: *(calls out as if in pain)* This is how our king honors a man! This is how our king honors a man!

(Once the two have crossed the stage twice, Haman runs off screaming in agony. Mordecai and horse exit as the stage lights go out.)

NARRATOR: And so Mordecai was honored. Haman lived through his embarrassment and was able to attend Queen Esther's dinner that night.

(Stage lights go on. The king and queen go to the table to sit. Haman stumbles over, exhausted. The king and queen appear to be enjoying a meal as they pantomime.)

KING XERXES: Another fine meal. Now, Queen Esther, tell me what you want!

QUEEN: All right, Your Highness. If you really care for me, you can save my people and me. You see, I am an Israelite, and we will all die soon by your royal order!

KING XERXES: *(slams fists on table, others get up and stand next to the table)* What! What are you talking about? Who is behind such a plot?

QUEEN: *(points to Haman)* Him! Haman is out to kill us!
(The king, in a rage, turns the table over and storms offstage. He speaks as he leaves.)

KING XERXES: I am so upset angry! I have to think! *(Departs the stage)*

(Haman turns to Esther and falls to his knees, accidentally knocking her down. As he reaches over to help her up, the king returns.)

KING XERXES: Get your hands off my queen! Now you're trying to attack Queen Esther right before my eyes!
(Looking offstage) Guards! Come and take Haman away!

(Guards enter and pull Haman's arms behind his back and then they speak.)

GUARD #1: Oh, king, we could hang Haman on the 75' tower he built to hang Mordecai!

GUARD #2: And Mordecai is the one who saved your life, king!

KING XERXES: What "sweet dessert" that would be! Go ahead; hang Haman from his own tower!

(Guards drag the screaming Haman offstage. The king and queen face each other and hold hands.)

KING XERXES: Queen Esther, this has been some day! *(He releases one of Esther's hands and begins to turn away from her. Both freeze as the narrator speaks.)*

NARRATOR: Esther was given everything that had been Haman's. When Esther told the king that Mordecai was really her cousin, Mordecai was promoted. But Esther wasn't about to let the king go yet. She must have been remembering Mordecai's words, "but could be that you were made queen for a time like this!"

(As the king starts to leave Esther grabs his other hand and falls to her knees to stop him. She looks up at this face.)

ESTHER: Please, Your Highness, you can put a stop to Haman's evil order to have all Israelites killed. But you must hurry because his letters have already gone throughout the entire Kingdom.

KING XERXES: All right, Queen Esther. Make a new law that will save the lives of your people. Use my signature to make it official.

(All extra players enter the stage in the background and cheer. They come forward and surround Esther. If physically able, stronger actors may carefully carry her off the stage in triumph.)

NARRATOR: The new order was written. The Children of Israel were saved from death. This event is remembered and celebrated today in the Feast of Purim (poo-rim). The feast of Purim retells how Queen Esther and her cousin Mordecai saved the Jews from the wicked Haman. If Esther had not had the courage to speak up for her people- for God's people- they might have been lost forever. The great plan God started with Abraham would have been stopped because of one man's pride and hatred. But perhaps, just perhaps, God placed Esther in this place at this time, for His special reasons... "for a time such as this!" Remember, God has been in control from the beginning. God has not left the Israelites, no matter how many times they have turned away from Him. Once again, God found an obedient person to carry out his plan. We must remember that this is the obedience God expects from us today, in our place, and in our time!

THE END

Nehemiah
Ezra 1-10, Nehemiah 1-9, 13,
and Malachi 1-4

CAST (Grouped by measure of involvement in play, most to least)
***Actors can double up on these parts.*

SPEAKING PARTS

Narrator-Teacher #1: Adult – will read connecting explanations between dialogues
Narrator-Teacher #2: Adult – will read connecting explanations between dialogues
Nehemiah: Adult male or older teen
Ezra: Adult male or older boy
Zerubbabel: Adult male or older teen**
Child #1: One of the youngest children**
Child #2: One of the youngest children**
Child #3: One of the youngest children**
Enemy #1: (Dressed in black) ** adult/older teen
Enemy #2: (Dressed in black)** adult/older teen
King: Any age male (will wear 2 different capes as 2 different kings in the play with 2 different crowns)
King's Messenger: Any age**
Malachi: Adult male or older teen
Man: Adult male or older teen who will speak with Malachi
Person #1: Any age**
Person #2: Any age**
Person #3: Any age**
Person #4: Any age**
Person #5: Any age**
Builders: Any age** (as many as possible- will be asked to sing)

NONSPEAKING PARTS

Wall Celebrators with Ezra: 5-10+
Sign carriers (3): Any age**
Children: Any age** 5-10+
Guards (2): Any age**
Officials (3-4): Any age**
Israelites: All extras**

STAGE

All scenes are set on a central stage area.

SETTING

The background will be neutral. Depending on the scene, the building blocks will be scattered around the back of the set to show disrepair or neatly stacked to show repairs in Jerusalem. As the play opens the blocks are scattered. Rocks are placed in the back and center part of the stage. The king's throne, which represents rich Babylon, is seen at the far right side of the stage during the whole play.

PROPS

- 2 large scrolls
- 3 different capes to represent 3 different kings
- 6 different signs:
    "ONE YEAR LATER"
    "DANGER-CONSTRUCTION!"
    "JERUSALEM CITY LIMITS" (*free standing and should look beat-up*)
    "WHILE BACK IN BABYLON . . ."
    "52 DAYS PASS"
    "THE TEMPLE IS COMPLETED!"
    "THE WALL IS COMPLETED!"
- 8-10 rocks for the alter – these can be balled up, spray-painted paper
- 30-40 light-weight building blocks (these can be painted – non-toxic- cardboard boxes)
- Bottles *(The bottles and following props will be needed to match the cast.)*
- Bows
- Building block that opens to hold bread
- Cymbals
- Donkey (decorated broomstick)
- Hammer
- Horns
- King's throne
- Large pieces of gold and silver vases or candlesticks
- Loose dirt in many small baggies
- Mural of the complete temple
- Raised platform
- Shields
- Shovel
- Trowel
- Hammer
- Small harps or stringed instruments of the day
- Speaking podium (one rock should be formed around a small step stool)
- Spears
- Swords

NOTE: If lighting cannot be controlled in order to move props and sets, use stage hands to move props in a quick and orderly way.

NEHEMIAH – The Play Begins

(The stage is full of children of all ages. The older ones will become builders once off-stage. All sit as they face the two narrator-teachers who tell the children their history as the children of Israel.)

NARRATOR-TEACHER #1: You've heard your parents tell you of how our ancestors enjoyed 120 golden years under King Saul, King David, and King Solomon. During those years, the boundaries of Israel grew larger, and the first temple was built for God in Jerusalem. We often call Jerusalem "The City of God".

NARRATOR-TEACHER #2: But then disobedient rulers came to the throne. The disobedience of these Children of Israel weakened the country. Israel divided into two kingdoms, a Northern Kingdom – called Israel – and a Southern Kingdom - called Judah. You've heard the saying "United we stand, divided we fall"? Well, that's exactly what happened to the Children of Israel, our ancestors.

NARRATOR-TEACHER #1: The first tragedy came when the Northern Kingdom - Israel, was completely destroyed by Assyrians in 722 B.C. This was very sad because we never heard from them again. When we talk about the "Ten Lost Tribes of Israel", that's who we mean.

NARRATOR-TEACHER #2: Then in 586 B.C., the Babylonians conquered the Southern Kingdom - Judah, and burned Jerusalem to the ground. Here they killed most of the men, women and children. Many of those who weren't killed were brought here to Babylon where they were held captive. Babylon is far from our homeland. It's in the area known as Mesopotamia.

CHILD #1: *(Stands and waves hand)* That sounds like how we were captives in Egypt. *(Child sits)*

NARRATOR-TEACHER #1: And to make it worse, the Babylonians burned Jerusalem and the temple to the ground, and afterwards they stole the gold and silver religious objects from the temple!

NARRATOR-TEACHER #2: The sad truth was that the land our God promised to Abraham, Isaac and Jacob, the Promised Land that Moses led our people to from exile in Egypt, was gone. We lost everything!

CHILD #2: *(stands)* So where was God? Why did God let this happen to His people a second time? *(sits)*

NARRATOR-TEACHER #1: Oh, child, God was there all along! God kept His promise. It was our people who forgot, or decided they didn't have to keep their end of the deal. They stopped following the laws God gave to Moses. They didn't worship God as He told them to, and they didn't follow the correct rules for temple sacrifices. They began to worship pagan idols and chose evil over good. It was very bad!

CHILD #3: *(stands)* What did God do? *(sits)*

NARRATOR-TEACHER #1: God did not give up on us. He sent messengers called prophets to warn the people to stop what they were doing and to remind them to follow His rules. These prophets were ordinary people, just like us. But the Israelites didn't listen to the prophets. Instead, they made fun of them. They didn't believe God's messages, no matter how many prophets were sent with God's specific words for them.

CHILD #1: *(stands)* Oh . . . Prophets like Jonah? Didn't he try to run away from the job God had for him? *(sits)*

NARRATOR-TEACHER #1: That's right! But in the end Jonah knew that he had to follow God's will because God was in control. Do any of you know any other prophets God used to try to reach us?

CHILD #2: *(stands)* Elijah and Elisha with the fire carriage and the wind that carried Elijah away? *(sits)*

NARRATOR-TEACHER #2: Very good! They spoke God's warnings in Israel, the Northern Kingdom.

CHILD #3: *(stands)* How about Isaiah and Jeremiah? *(sits)*

NARRATOR-TEACHER #1: Right again! These two prophets spoke to the people and rulers in Judah, the Southern Kingdom.

NARRATOR-TEACHER #2: You see, God covered all the bases.

CHILD #1: Wow! *(stands)* And they still didn't pay attention? *(sits)*

NARRATOR-TEACHER #1: No, they didn't. The sad part is that wasn't the first time our people messed up and forgot the rules. God waited until he had seen enough, and then he punished them. He heard their cries for help and rescued them in his own time. The people tried to live the right way, but it never lasted. Part of the problem occurred when they found themselves living near people who worshiped other gods, and not the God of the children of Israel. Some of God's children even lived in the same houses where other gods were worshiped. Some began to lose respect for God's temple and forgot the one true God who had seen them through so much.

CHILD #2: *(stands)* How could they be so blind? *(sits)*

(Zerubbabel walks in silently from the back and walks towards the group as the narrator speaks.)

NARRATOR-TEACHER #2: No one is perfect. Each of us is weak. That is why we must remember our true God. Only He can protect and save us. And tomorrow we'll be starting over again. Tomorrow we head back to our homeland, the land God gave to us years ago, the same land we lost because of our disobedience. Jerusalem, here we come! Oh! *(Points to Zerubbabel)* Here comes Zerubbabel! He will be one of our leaders. *(Zerubbabel walks to front of stage where he faces the children.)*

ZERUBBABBEL: Are you all ready to begin our travels tomorrow? Are you ready to see the homeland of your parents and grandparents?

CHILDREN: *(All cheer and say "yes")*

ZERUBABBEL: *(to narrator-teachers)* Do you know whose footsteps we'll be following? Who followed God and led our people 1,400 years ago?

CHILD #3: *(jumping up)* Father Abraham! *(sits)*

ZERUBABBEL: Do you know the first thing we'll do once we arrive?

CHILD #1: *(stands)* We're going to build an altar and offer sacrifices to God! *(remains standing)*

ZERUBABBEL: Yes! Are you ready to follow God?

CHILDREN: *(unison)* YES, we are! *(They jump and skip off the stage with Narrator #2 and Zerubabbel, Narrator #1 remains onstage as stage lights go off.)*

NOTE: Narrator #2 readings are now complete.

(Builders walk onstage, and as lights go on, each goes to the rock pile and picks up a rock. Narrator begins to speak as Zerubabbel walks on stage to the pile of rocks, gets a rock and leads others builders with rocks to the front left corner of the stage where they build an altar. They all walk offstage as the sign carriers walk across the stage carrying the signs, "One year later," and "Construction area.")

NARRATOR #1: The first group of Israelites returned to their homeland about 539 B.C. where they found their homeland in ruins. Zerubabbel, who became governor, was one of the leaders. They built an altar and offered sacrifices to God. Other people were living in their homeland, but the Israelites were brave and resettled. It was a year, though, before they got around to building the foundation for the new temple in Jerusalem.

(Zerubabbel and builders pick up building blocks. They hum quietly as they lay half of the foundation. The narrator continues while they're building.)

NARRATOR #1 continues: The people rejoiced when the foundation was completed. *(Trumpets blow and cymbals crash in the background).* Building plans rarely go without a catch. As the building continued, the enemies of the Israelites showed up. They appeared to want to help rebuild Jerusalem, but actually they were there to sabotage the reconstruction in an effort to keep Israel weak.

(Enemies enter and stand watching the builders work. A scroll is quickly paced on the ground.)

NARRATOR # 1 continues: This angered the enemy so much that they wrote a letter to the new king, Artaxerxes, King of Persia. King Artaxerxes now ruled over the entire area following the fall of the Assyrians and Babylonians. He showed compassion and allowed the uprooted people to return to their homes with the promise they would pay taxes to him.

(Enemies run up to the King, and one unrolls the scroll and reads aloud.)

ENEMY #1: Dear King Artaxerxes, FYI! We tell you this news because we think you are so wonderful. The Israelites who left your country to go back to Jerusalem are rebuilding that terrible city. Once the walls and city are rebuilt they will not pay taxes to you anymore! Plus, just look at their police records! These people are real trouble makers! That's why Jerusalem was destroyed in the first place! Signed, Your Friends.

(The King puts hands on face and looks shocked.)

KING ARTAXERXES: *(to king's messenger)* **Go, immediately, and tell the builders to stop!**

(King freezes in place. Messenger runs with the scroll towards builders who become animated again, and pantomimes a message about the building. They immediately freeze in place and the messenger walks off the stage with the scroll. Stage lights go off and the second cape is put on the seated king to represent a change in kings.)

NARRATOR #1 : *(Stage lights come on)* **When King Darius took over as King of Persia, God told the prophets in Jerusalem to urge the people to resume building. Again, the enemy reported to the king.**

(Builders resume work as the king's messenger quietly walks on stage and stands next to King Darius. The enemy speaks again.)

ENEMY #2: King Darius, the Israelites claim to be God's servants. They are rebuilding the temple that was built by Israel's great King Solomon 500 years ago. They say their God was angry and punished them by letting King Nebuchadnezzar of Babylon destroy the first temple. Their God allowed them to be captured and taken to Babylon. God also let their captors take the temple's gold and silver for placement in our Babylonian temple. These Israelites also say that the Babylonian King Cyrus ordered them to rebuild the temple where it stood before. King Darius, could you check the records to see if this is true?

KING DARIUS: *(King turns and speaks to his messenger)* **Messenger! Go now and find the answer to the question. Bring the answer back to me.**

(King pantomimes talking with those around him while the King's messenger runs offstage. He grabs a scroll, runs back on stage, and hands the scroll to the King. The King stands up, opens the scroll, looks shocked, and drops his hands to his sides.)

KING DARIUS continues: The Israelites are correct! The records say that King Cyrus directed them to rebuild the temple and it also says *(softly)* **to return the gold and silver.**
(He trembles as if in fear.) **I want NO ARGUMENTS! Let the Children of Israel rebuild and DON'T slow them down! Or YOU'LL BE SORRY!!!**
(King and all others walk off the stage as the stage lights go off.)

NARRATOR #1: The temple was finally complete about 516 B.C.

(Mural of temple, or overhead shot may be made visible. Blow trumpets offstage.)

NARRATOR #1: People continued to return from Babylon in waves. Ezra was one who returned. He was one of the experts who explained the Laws of Moses, or Torah, to the people.

(Ezra enters mid-stage and kneels in prayer. Stage lights go on.)

NARRATOR #1: A teacher like Ezra was called a scribe. Ezra truly enjoyed his work helping the people understand God's words. Years earlier, God gave Ezra the desire to teach people how to

worship. The young ones who now saw the new temple rejoiced while the elders who remembered the first temple cried when they recalled the greatness that could not be duplicated. While Ezra was filled with joy and thanksgiving for God's blessings, he was shocked to see a broken down altar and golden idols. He saw the people committing the same sins that got them exiled in the first place. He feared their punishment again, so he organized servants for the temple and told them to fast and to pray to God. Ezra turned to God.

EZRA: *(on knees)* Oh, God! You alone are in control, no matter who rules over us. We must remember that you, again, freed us.

(Persons #1- #5 come on stage, see Ezra, walk towards them and listen as he prays. They look confused, then hug each other with apparent fear. Then they quietly pray in agreement with Ezra.

EZRA continues in prayer: You are the one, great God, who has allowed us to rebuild the temple in Jerusalem. You told the king and authorities to help us. Lord, you are just, but here we are before you already beginning to turn against your wishes.

PERSON #1: Oh Ezra, you are right.

PERSON #2: We have disobeyed God!

PERSON #3: We will listen to you.

PERSON #4: We want to do God's will.

PERSON #5: We want to please our one and only God!

EZRA: Good. You have heard. I hope God hears us! Let us rest today. I hear a new group is arriving tomorrow from Babylon. Remember to honor our God!

(Stage lights go off as characters leave the stage. Stagehands scatter building blocks to represent the broken down city walls. Sign carrier walks across stage with "WHILE BACK IN BABYLON" sign. Second King enters and sits on the throne wearing the second cape. Stage lights go on and Nehemiah enters stage and paces back and forth in obvious distress as he talks to himself.)

NEHEMIAH: The walls are still broken down 70 years after the temple was finished! The gates are still burned and not replaced, even after all this time that my people have been in Jerusalem! I just can't stand to think about it! I must do something!
(Falls to his knees in anguished prayer.)

NARRATOR #1: It looks like God has done it again! God has put a bit of knowledge and desire in an average person's heart.

NEHEMIAH: *(Looking up in loud prayer)* Oh, Dear God! I am your servant, Great God! I believe if we obey your laws, we can always turn to you, no matter where we are. You know that I am a trusted servant of the Persian King here in Babylon. Please let the king allow me to go to Jerusalem to help rebuild the walls! I have such a strong desire to go and help! My heart beats faster and faster when I think of it! *(Rises and walks over to the king.)*

KING ARTAXERXES: Nehemiah! What is wrong with you? I've never seen you so upset. Tell me what is wrong!

NEHEMIAH: *(Shaking with fear)* With your permission, oh King, please send me to Jerusalem so that I can rebuild the city where my ancestors are buried.

KING ARTAXERXES: Well, we'll have to work out the details. But yes, you may go!

NEHEMIAH: Oh, and I'll also need material for building. May I have your help with this?

KING ARTAXERXES: Of course! You may also take army officers and troops to assist you. *(Nehemiah bows to the King and rushes offstage. King walks off. Nehemiah re-enters from one side of the stage and officials enter from the other side of the stage. Nehemiah carries building gear: trowel, hammer, shovel as he walks over to officials who pantomime anger and rejection of him as they quickly exits the stage. Nehemiah walks towards building blocks.)*

NARRATOR #1: Not all the people had good feeling towards Nehemiah's work. Some of the officials were angry because they did not want to see any help go to the people of Israel. The first thing Nehemiah did was to survey the walls of the city of Jerusalem.

(Nehemiah walks around with his hand to his head as if looking in the distance for Jerusalem. When he reaches the pile of scattered blocks he stops, sees a donkey – broom donkey – and "rides" it all around the stage as if surveying the scattered blocks. His looks are of shock and dismay. Stage goes dark. A stagehand now places the sign, "JERUSALEM CITY LIMITS", by the loose building blocks and places the rock podium – with small stepstool inside – in the center of the stage.)

(Stage lights go on and he dismounts the donkey, handing it offstage. Nehemiah meets the Israelites as they enter stage. Persons #1- #5 enter. Builders enter. Nehemiah climbs up on the rock platform.)

NEHEMIAH: My people, Jerusalem walls are a mess! The city gates are down and burned. Wherever I went on my tour this morning I saw so much in ruins. While I was working for the King of Babylon I heard rumors of how bad it was, which made me feel sad. But then God touched my heart with a dream. God gave me the desire to come back and help rebuild Jerusalem so we could feel good about our city! God gave me this message to rebuild. To top it off, God softened the king's heart so much that he gave me permission to return to Jerusalem and willingly offered building materials.

PERSON #1: What are we waiting for?

(Person #1 turns around and beckons to the audience as he rushes over to the scattered blocks. He starts piling them up as the narrator continues. Enemies run on stage and pantomime throwing insults at the builders as the narrator and Nehemiah next speak.)

NARRATOR #1: Again, the local enemies insult the children of Israel. This time Nehemiah speaks while they continue the insults.

NEHEMIAH: *(to enemies)* We are servants of God. He will see that our work succeeds. *(Remains watching)*

(The builders continue as enemies make negative hand motions towards builders.)

NARRATOR #1: Priests, Levites, and others built the wall while their enemies made fun of them. The enemies grew angry at the people when the work did not stop. *(Enemies begin to lightly poke at the workers.)* They began to fight so guards had to be stationed. *(Two guards enter the stage with spears, shields and bows. The first stands guard with the builders. The second is located on the other side by the enemies.)*
NARRATOR #1 continues: Constant prayer was heard along with work songs as the workers build.

BUILDERS: *(sing in a rhyming way)* So much rubble for us to haul! Hallelujah! Worn out and weary, will we finish this wall? Hallelujah.

(Builders continue singing quietly.)

NARRATOR #1: The enemy planned more attacks.

(One of the enemies sneaks up behind the builders as the second guard comes up behind him, tapping him on the shoulder. The enemy jumps and runs off. Builders turn around to see the guard, and Nehemiah is standing next to the guard.)

NEHEMIAH: *(to builders)* Don't be afraid of attacks. God will help us complete our work. Since we are so spread out, listen for a trumpet sound. If you hear it, follow the sound. God will fight for us.

(Persons #1 - #5 take turns using the spears, shields and bows.)

NARRATOR #1: Nehemiah had half the men work while the other half carried spears, shields, and bows as protection.
("Persons" approach Nehemiah from the other side; he turns to face them. Builders appear to complete wall and walk around wiping off their hands. They stand back and admire it. The stage lights go off and everyone leaves the stage. Stage lights go on. Two sign carriers walk across the stage – "52 DAYS PASS" and "THE TEMPLE WALL IS COMPLETED!" All extra characters come on stage, point to the signs and cheer. As the narrator reads, they continue to slap each other's backs and show physical expressions of joy. The enemies enter the stage, standing at the left side, stomp their feet in disgust and exit.)

NARRATOR #1: By now the enemies feel as if they have been defeated in their attempt to keep Jerusalem from being rebuilt. They realize that the God of the Israelites must truly have been there to help the Jewish people. All they could do was watch the priests, Levites, temple guards, musicians, workers and ordinary people return and settle in Judah. Once again, the people's minds become more focused on God's law.

(Ezra enters the stage with a scroll and stands on the rock podium. They turn to hear what Ezra, the priest, has to say to them, from the writings of Moses.)

EZRA: *(opens scroll)* Our God, the one true God of the universe, is great!

(As the narrator talks Ezra mouths the words as though he were preaching.)

NARRATOR #1: Ezra told the people important guidelines from writings of Moses.

ALL PEOPLE: *(shout)* Amen, Amen!
(Then bow down with their faces to the ground and began to cry loudly.)

NARRATOR #1: As Ezra continued the people began to weep. They realized how bad they have been. They were not following all of God's laws. They felt so ashamed.

EZRA: Do not cry! This day is special for God. He is thrilled to see you learning His laws and praising Him!

(Nehemiah walks over to Ezra)

NEHEMIAH: Listen to Ezra! This day is special for God. He will make you happy and strong. Do not cry, but go and eat and drink. Enjoy yourselves, BUT, remember to share with someone who does not have food! Remember God's laws! *(Ezra gets down from podium and mingles in the crowd.)*

NARRATOR #1: The people did just that. *(People pantomime conversation.)* They enjoyed having fellowship with each other.

(Stage lights go off. Ezra gets back on podium. People are handed baggies filled with dirt. People sit around the podium to listen to him and stage lights go on.)

NARRATOR #1: The next day they listened to more of Ezra's teachings. They learned more and celebrated as God's words directed them to do all week. Then it was time to confess their sins. *(All stand up)* They would not eat and they showed their sorrow by putting dirt on their clothes. *(Sprinkle loose dirt from bags.)* They stood listening to Ezra for three hours, then confessed their sins and worshipped God.

(Group members walk to the front of the stage, face the audience and kneel in silent prayer.)

EZRA: Oh Great God, Your name is glorious! May it always be praised above all names! You are God. No one else is! You created the highest skies and the stars that shine throughout the heavens. You made the earth and everything on it. You made the waters and everything in them. You alone give life and all of your creations worship you. You are the One who chose Abraham. You made a covenant with him to give his descendants the Promised Land. You were true and kept your promise. No matter what our ancestors did, you still loved them. You showed compassion by staying with them. When they became so disobedient to you, you handed them over their enemies, but you still heard their cries. And because of your love, you sent deliverers to rescue them. Over and over you saved them. For years you were patient and you sent prophets to speak your warnings. But they did not listen. Oh God, remember how we suffered under the Assyrians in Babylon? We are again like slaves when the kings take our harvest. They still treated us like animals!

NEHEMIAH: *(Walks to podium rock. Ezra climbs down and to the side of the stage before Nehemiah arrives and climbs up.)* As governor I declare that we make an agreement. We must all agree to obey the laws that God gave Moses for us to follow. We must also agree to accept God's punishment if we do not obey those laws. In no way can we allow ourselves to be

influenced by other people who worship other gods. We must be true to our one and only God.
(People cheer)

(As the next people speak, several wall celebrators leave the stage to get musical instruments.)

PERSON #1: We will honor our God!

PERSON #2: We will take care of the temple!

PERSON #3: Praise God!

NARRATOR #1: More joy was to come, for it was time to dedicate the city wall. The children of Israel came from all over Judah. Look, here comes Ezra leading the first group!

(Wall celebrators with instruments enter the stage making joyful sounds as they and line up behind Ezra. Everyone joins in and they all march back and forth across the stage celebrating with music.)

NEHEMIAH: (*Walks to join remaining celebrators as they approach Ezra.)*
Ezra! Praise our Lord! What a wonderful day He has given us!

EZRA: (*Waving and calling back)* Governor Nehemiah, remember always to praise our one and only God! Remember the agreement we signed! We are under the Lord our God. Always, and in all ways, remember that promise!

(Extra cast members separate and some follow Nehemiah off the stage while others follow Ezra off the stage in a different direction. If possible, have the groups walk out through the audience making musical noise as the narrator concludes.)

PEOPLE: Praise our God! He is great! He is good! Praise Him always!

NARRATOR #1: The children of Israel were very happy. They had returned home to Judah from exile in Babylon. The temple was rebuilt under God-fearing leaders like Nehemiah. God led men like Ezra to bring back correct temple service and the understanding of His words. Though the Ark of the Covenant with the original Ten Commandments had disappeared when Jerusalem's temple was destroyed, there was a spot for it in the new temple. But more importantly, God was back in their hearts. They heard God and followed His laws again. They offered the right sacrifices. They took care of each other, and they stayed away from other gods that some people worshiped. Would the children of Israel stick to their agreement to worship only their one true God this time?

(Lights dim and all is silent.)

 NARRATOR #1: Time flies. 100 years after the first group of exiles returned to Jerusalem in 536 BC, who does God send? Even after the people had returned to their homeland from Babylon, God again saw the need to send one... more... prophet. His name was Malachi.
(Malachi enters and addresses the audience. Stage lights go on.)

MALACHI: Oh it is so good that Jerusalem, the city walls, and the temple are standing again. But...I see the children of Israel slipping backwards. They are not honoring God like they know they should. Now, God has sent me to tell them He knows what's happening. They're losing their commitment to worship and greed is setting in. The priests are showing contempt for God and it's seen in their poor offerings to Him.

MAN: *(seated in audience, or joining audience from behind)* Oh, Malachi! We've heard that before, even before we were taken into exile in Babylon. The prophet named Isaiah kept talking about God's greatness and how He was merciful. He hated idolatry and rewarded obedience. We've heard it all! Isaiah even described a Savior who would come and save us from our oppressors!

MALACHI: And how has that news changed the way you live?

MAN: Well, it does look like we're just about back where we started. It's really seen in how our obedience and worship have cooled off towards God. We're taking God's blessings for granted.

MALACHI: We've all been created by the same great God, right? So why can't we live as He expects us to? Just what do you think God requires of us?

MAN: The prophet, Micah, summed up God's expectations for us, "to be just, to be merciful, and to walk humbly with our God."

MALACHI: But the people don't do it. They argue with God and demand to know where the God of justice is. They need to know that God promises to send his messenger who will prepare a way for him.   God says that the Lord we are seeking will come to his temple. He will be the messenger of the covenant, and he *will* come.

MAN: And what will that be like for us all?

MALACHI: Oh, it will be like a refiner's fire as He comes near. The day is coming when the evildoers will be stubble and set on fire. But you must remember God still loves us because even though we can't keep our promise to God, God does not change. God still says that he is still here if we choose him. For those who love God, they will rise with healing and leap like calves released from their stalls.

MAN: Ah, but we are just men of dust, and he is God. God knows what we need. We need a savior because we just can't do it on our own.

MALACHI: God says he will send the prophet Elijah, and if hearts don't turn to God, those people will be cursed.

MAN: God has blessed us so much and put up with so much.   It's amazing that God still longs for his people to love him and that he promises to help us.

MALACHI: Only God can save us. Only God, who has never left us, can change the course of all history and make things right.

(Lights dim and Malachi and the man leave the stage.)

NARRATOR #1: Malachi was the last prophet to speak God's words to the people until God sent the prophet, John the Baptist, 400 years later. In those 400 years of silence the children of Israel had God's written word as told by Moses and the prophets. The people continue to struggle as they wait for their promised deliverer. There is hope because God has not finished with the people yet. God *will* have the last word.

THE END